SAX MAN

BY TED SCHWARZ

red giant books

Author's Apology

Okay, when you read a biography you expect the story to follow a set pattern roughly equivalent to the subject's path through life. Sometimes it starts with the subject's birth. Sometimes it starts at a high point or low point of his/her career. However it is done, the story is linear, and since the story of Maurice "Sax Man" Reedus, Jr. is one of many I have written over the years, it would seem logical to expect this to be no different. However, if that is the case, you are wrong.

The Sax Man has lived his life like the music he plays—as a series of riffs and flourishes, each a bridge to the previous or the one that follows. Some times there seems to be a cohesive score, albeit one Reedus seems to have mislaid and is searching to rediscover. At other times you realize that he has stepped up to the microphone on the stage of life with no idea how he got there, where he's going, or what the words might mean. That is when he goes from lyrics that make sense to the observer and a sophisticated scat whose origins are uncertain, whose ending is beyond comprehension, yet whose musical journey fascinates, shocks, and delights.

I embarked on the research, the interviews, and the street photography sessions needed to try and tell the Sax Man's story several years ago. I had no idea what I would be encountering other than it was obvious that the Sax Man is a unique yet integral part of the fabric of the city of Cleveland, Ohio. His life has been filled with love, laughter, and a quirkiness that has always set him apart from the estimated 130,000 people a week who are embraced by the sound of his music. He has been feted and cursed, a herald who appears outside every sporting event, in front of the cluster of theaters at Playhouse Square when the curtain is about to rise on one or another touring Broadway shows, and in the midst of Public Square, the crossroads of downtown.

Clevelanders, I discovered, embrace the Sax Man's fantasy that "everybody knows me," though the truth is that no one really has known the Sax Man. That was why I began following the unusual musician with a camera and tape recorder, documenting his presence in the city, documenting the impact of his music, and asking him all those questions your mother, like my own, probably told you were not polite to ask a stranger.

That the music the Sax Man cannot read [he has dyslexia], the solos that made him memorable to some of the jazz greats over the years, all are a part of telling his story. Yet each stands alone. Each is a riff, a flourish, a passage that can rise to genius as it flows from his heart through his mouthpiece and out his horn. A traditonal narrative no more does the Sax Man justice then does dismissing prolific geniuses like Duke Ellington and Billy Strayhorn *mere* song writers.

I may not even know the song, but if I hear it in my head, I can play it."

—*Maurice Reedus, Jr.*

Introduction

Riffs on the Life and Times of Cleveland's Most Famous Street Musician

Maurice Reedus, Jr. was hungry when he arrived at the House of Blues, the Cleveland concert venue on the edge of East 4th Street and Euclid Avenue. There was supposed to be food backstage after the first sound check, and he knew he was allowed to take some. After all, on the outside marquee was his name and that of the first band with which he had gone on national and international tours, Sly, Slick & Wicked. At that moment, though, he would settle for cookies and milk he could buy from the CVS drugstore on East 9th Street if it would give him an extra few minutes to play his saxophone for passers-by. That would hopefully be all the time he needed to get enough money to pay for one more night in the inexpensive, university area hotel room where he was living until a subsidized apartment opened in the Ernest Bohn Towers, one of the near downtown Cleveland Metropolitan Housing Authority buildings.

Reedus had thought he was getting paid for the gig that night. All the musicians who had gathered for the concert being filmed had played throughout the nation and, in many cases, throughout the world. Minimum fees and expenses had been arranged before they left their homes for Cleveland and Maurice assumed he was being treated like the others. After all, playing with many of the musicians was how he had started his career. He had been a back-up musician, a stand-up comic, and though this was to be his special night, he had no ego. He assumed—some observers felt rightfully—that he would receive the same fee as the other professionals. He didn't need or want to be a star. He just wanted to be part of the horn section, one of the conga players, a musician among musicians delighting the largest audience—an estimated 800 people—before which he had performed in many years.

The expectations were understandable. After all, it was his name literally in lights, and his life the film crew had been recording these many months. But earlier in the day there had been no mistaking the voice of the man working the hotel front desk who informed Reedus that he was almost out of time to pay his $60 bill for another day. And there was no mistaking what he felt was the seeming hollowness of the producer's promise that Maurice, locally known as The Sax Man, would be taken care of. After all, he was the "star."

Maurice Reedus never wanted to be famous. He never wanted to be rich. He just wanted to delight the public with the sound of his music and to be treated with dignity and respect. Certainly he was thrilled by the night's gathering of some of the top musicians in the country planning to perform one more time together with Maurice after as many as 40 years apart. Even when they went their separate ways over the decades, they shared the same work ethic, the same respect for the audience. But that night it seemed to Reedus he was the only musician the production company though was expendable. His name was literally in lights on the Euclid Avenue entrance to the Cleveland House of Blues. He was the only performer who had been asked to promote the show by making appearances on local radio and television. His story was the reason an estimated $250,000 had been raised to produce The Sax Man documentary.

But at that moment when Maurice arrived to get ready for the show, he was hungry. He was also broke. It was not an unusual predicament for him though he had thought that having his name in lights might be a nice accompaniment to having some cash in his pocket after so many months of being the subject of a documentary on which the producers would be building their own reputation.

Chapter One

The Sax Man Cometh

"By and large, Jazz has always been like the kind of a man you wouldn't want your daughter to associate with."—Duke Ellington

How it came about

The story of the Sax Man began with an erroneous assumption on my part. It was 4:30 in the afternoon and I was hurrying from my office in the City Club Building in order to reach Tower City and the Rapid Transit that would take me home. As I approached East 4th Street, by then in the final phase of its conversion to downtown Cleveland's newest and most elaborate apartment, entertainment, and dining center, I heard a saxophone being played in a graffiti-covered doorway. The music was the theme song of a long ago prime time children's television show since banished to the purgatory of the non-network insomniac hours where inexpensive reruns from the 1950s and 1960s vie for viewer attention with infomercials touted by "I thought he had died"former celebrities.

The man who was playing the saxophone was as eccentric as his choice of music and the place where he had chosen to serenade mostly uncaring office workers more concerned with beating the Rush Hour traffic than looking at what presumably was a panhandler with a better gimmick than most. The Sax Man was well dressed, tall, and so lean that he looked as if someone left an old but still serviceable three piece designer suit draped over a broomstick. He wore sunglasses and a beret, the latter tilted at a jaunty, seemingly casual angle achievable only after minutes of careful preening and positioning in front of a mirror. The final effect was more 1960's Beat Poet on Open Mike Night from a long ago counter-culture coffee shop than a musician's solo performance, yet it was obvious that the Sax Man was a serious musician, if only by the standards he set for himself.

I kept expecting to be asked for a few dollars "so I can get something to eat, man." If he was an experienced hustler he might add a hard luck story that some of the regular passers-by encouraged for what they deemed their entertainment value. The only ones I had heard in recent weeks were from a beggar who worked East 8th Street, the pretentiously named alley that runs from Euclid to Prospect Avenues. Every few days he announced a new crisis requiring the acquisition of other people's spare change. Most recently he lamented that his mother-in-law had been kidnapped by boxer Mike Tyson and he needed to pay the ransom.

There was also the beggar in a wheelchair who worked Public Square before such characters were banished by the increased security that came with the opening of the Horseshoe Casino. Some people handed the guy money without really looking at him. Others mentioned this or that doctor, usually at the Cleveland Clinic, who they thought could help him regain mobility. He thanked each of them, often managing a tear sliding touchingly down one cheek. What he did not do was let them see him get out of his wheelchair and rent it for an hour or two to another hustler while he went for a walk, his body stiff from sitting too long.

The Sax Man was different in that he didn't seem to have a story and the horn he played was not a gimmick. He kept his instrument case open and some people dropped in pocket change or opened their wallets to give him folding money, but he never looked inside the case, never seemed to see the people who either appreciated his musical efforts or yielded to what I still thought was his hustle.

I realized that if he was "real," the Sax Man was obviously all about his music. I wanted to see him again but didn't know if he stayed in one location or wandered other areas of the city. I also assumed he had no permanent address that he might stay in one.

Over the next week or two I began walking the streets of Cleveland, trying to use my ears to find the Sax Man in locations other than East 4th. I learned that where he played varied with his mood, the time of day, whether or not there were sporting events in the city, and what shows were being performed in the theaters of Playhouse Square. He proved to be a traveling busker, playing outside the fast food restaurants along East 9th Street between Euclid and Superior Avenues, playing on Public Square, playing by the Euclid Avenue entrance of the Old Arcade and across the street from the main library, playing wherever people passed. He talked with no one unless they spoke to him, and even then he could be so lost in listening to the impact of urban acoustics on the sound of his sax that he never heard their questions, never heard their good wishes.

I took lunch hour and afternoon walks with a camera, a notebook, and a tape recorder in my gadget bag. Over the years I have been a freelance photographer, one of my specialties being stories of unusual people that ultimately appeared in publications ranging from the American Family Circle to Germany's Stern to Cleveland's alternative weeklies. I didn't know if the Sax Man might be more interesting than just the subject of a quick photograph. What I knew was that he was clean, well dressed, and obviously not homeless. And I saw that during those few moments when someone spoke to him or he greeted a regular passer-by, he was friendly, articulate, and not the type of downtown denizen who has conversations with people who exist only inside their minds. As a result I reached a point where I felt compelled to introduce myself, to ask the Sax Man for an interview whenever he wasn't playing his sax. He agreed and we met for what became more than 75 hours of recordings.

The Sax Man took me into his past, from the projects in which he once lived to the world of Blind Eddie Smoot's Courageous Young Men to a tour of the United States culminating in playing before 80,000 people, to the almost clichéd use of recreational drugs when playing with one band or another, to the women he found seductive, seducible, and ultimately mad as hell when they realized that a major emotional commitment from the Sax Man might range from an hour or two to no more than a couple of weeks.

I spent several months doing both brief and lengthy interviews as well as photographing the Sax Man all over Cleveland, my hundreds of still photos eventually matched by hours of digital recording by a documentary crew whose members discovered the Sax Man by chance just as I had done.

The Sax Man proved to be intensely desirous of the attention only a camera can provide. I had seen the same reaction from the best professional models with whom I worked during a time in my life when I was a freelance commercial photographer. A reasonably attractive young woman would come to my studio in order to pose for one advertisement or another. The photographs I was to take were for clients ranging from clothing specialty shops to catalog sales departments. The clients always assumed that whatever they were selling would move faster if displayed with a pretty young woman wearing it, holding it, or both.

The models understood this. They knew they were selling their own appearance as much as the product, and all of them were comfortable looking into the camera lens and smiling to appeal to the potential buyer of whatever was being sold. Every photo of just about every model used commercially in that manner was unusually attractive, what some cosmetics manufacturers were then calling "model pretty."

There was a handful of models who were different. They would arrive with the usual accessories, from changes of clothing to specialized make-up kits. They knew how to stand and sit in ways that were slimming and effectively draw the viewer's eye. But there was more to them. These were young women who had learned to use the camera's lens to create a visual interaction with the viewer that was as intimate as a lover's kiss. They were the models who experienced Cleveland as the first major step to a modeling career in New York, and from there to an international career in London, Paris, and Milan.

The Sax Man was not a model. He did not radiate the through-the-lens eroticism I occasionally experienced with one of the young women who posed for me in those long ago sessions. But what he did have was a stage presence I had encountered with what I previously considered legitimate performers. His clothing was clean and pressed. His movements were casual yet practiced. And when he played, he seemed to be simultaneously aware of his audience of passers-by and oblivious to their reactions to him, much like being on a stage, performing in a spotlight. The light is too bright for the eyes to adjust both to the performer's surroundings and the dimly lit audience.

Years earlier I photographed performers ranging from comic Bill Cosby to actress Jayne Kennedy to singer Karen Carpenter and her brother Richard. They all had a certain physical style and persona on stage quite apart from who they were when not before an audience.

The Sax Man was no different. The man I photographed stand-ing by one or another active downtown streets was not the same as the man I saw riding the bus from his apartment, then walking to whatever corner he determined would be that day's stage. One had a style and a presence that had to have been learned through experi-ence. The other was like any other Clevelander walking to work. One stood out, catching your attention. The other faded into the pace of the city.

The Sax Man was not seductive in the manner of those long ago models, but he seemed to instinctively understand the effects I was trying to achieve, posing against graffiti-covered boards nailed tempo-rarily over entrances to buildings undergoing interior renovation, and standing on the edge of the roof of my building, using his sax to sere-nade the city in the light of the rising sun.

Once again I made an assumption, this time that I would tell his story as I had written the lives of other men and women, in a linear fashion—when he was born, entered school, experienced his parents' divorce, when he took up playing music, etc. Then, when the first draft was completed, men and women from the Sax Man's life suddenly decided they wanted to talk about him, really talk, and not just say nice things they thought I wanted to hear. By the time I had detailed inter-views with musicians, producers, friends, enemies, past acquaintances, and numerous others, I realized I had heard about a totally different in-dividual radically different from the first.

Those conversations were followed by my being taught the histo-ry of local musicians and other entertainers facing a racial divide in Cleveland's nightspots. Blacks, no matter how famous and brilliant as musicians, played in one group of clubs while whites were relegated to another. [The rare mixed race locations were called Black and Tan, the most popular being Leo's Casino] Blacks in Cleveland knew about all the clubs, knew where the doors were open to them and knew where just trying to enter a whites-only club could lead to a bouncer, out of control patron, and/or security guard would toss them in the street.

Eventually blacks patronized some of the most exciting clubs of any type. Among others there was Leo's Casino and Bob Harris's Sir Rah House, the latter both a traditional club and a weekend afternoon gathering place for everything from teen bands starting their careers to local and national professional groups, all playing together, challenging one another, and all earning their chops.

Publicity for black acts and clubs where management welcomed all races came from the pages of Cleveland's Call & Post, the Pittsburgh Courier, and the Chicago Defender, as well as such "black" radio stations as WJMO and WABQ. There might also be advertising and reviews in the daily Cleveland News, Press, and Plain Dealer, and in the weekly Sun papers. But Cleveland blacks understood that unless an act—black or white—was promoted in their media and not just the white press, they were not welcome in the audience.

The racism in Cleveland and a number of other cities shattered some professionals, forcing them to perform for little or no money, little publicity, and little chance to prove their potential before a large audience. Some of the performers decided the effort was not worth the reward. They abandoned the stage for everything from menial labor (Famed singer Jimmy Scott worked in the laundry of the Hotel Cleveland during a time in his life others would have considered mid-career. Unlike so many others, though, he eventually returned to the stage and performing throughout the world.) to working on the fringes of the business—record promotion, being a DJ, running a record store, and the like.

The Sax Man is not the story of a lost talent, walking the streets after being ignored by the mainstream media. It is not a traditional biography filled with interviews with everyone from his third grade teacher to his 7th cousin five times removed to the high school band director who never thought he would succeed in life. Instead it is the

story of a musician who followed his dreams, embracing eccentric-
ity like a "fashionista" embraces the current season's clothing styles,
ignoring his musician father's advice, drifting in and out of gigs with
one or another bands, and ultimately taking pride in a non-tradition-
al lifestyle, an ever changing audience, and the fame that comes from
in-your-face contact with men, women, and children who know his
name but not the man himself.

It is also the story of a handful of peripheral players in the Sax
Man's story, from a brief but emotional encounter with the famed
Count Basie to a relative by marriage who began his mastery of
music while in jail. And in the end, when the words of his critics
seemed destined to overwhelm him, he became the star of a documen-
tary and had the honor to play for the first inductees of the R&B Hall
of Fame before returning to the streets where his horn provides a symbi-
otic relationship with the car horns, rush hour stop-and-go squealing
brakes and screeching tires of the urban theater.

Chapter Two

Music Will Out

1960: Somewhere on Cleveland's east Side

I heard the clarinet before I saw the boy who was playing the instrument. He was perhaps nine years old and sitting near the edge of the roof of an aged apartment building on one of the streets just off East 79th in Cleveland, Ohio. The sky was overcast, the steady drizzle of a chilling Spring rain had fallen an hour or two earlier, leaving the city feeling wrapped in a just washed, lightweight jacket removed too soon from a Laundromat dryer. The boy on the roof seemed oblivious to the day's chilling dampness, though his clothes appeared inadequate for keeping him warm. His focus was on the music, and he played with a maturity of sound that indicated a commitment to practice unexpected from someone so young playing in a neighborhood where no matter how hard working a family might be, they were often one paycheck from an eviction.

Outsiders who drove through the neighborhood with their car doors securely locked, their windows rolled up, did not consider the area a"nice" one. And in truth the apartment buildings, such as the one on whose roof the boy was sending the sounds of jazz into the mid-morning sky, might be classed as "war zones" by the tenants.

This was not an area of gang warfare as some suburbanites probably suspected. And this was not a street where undercover cops fought with juvenile gangs and doors were closed with multiple locks. Inside these buildings armies of cockroaches, bedbugs, rodents, and uncaring landlords were pitted against families trying to put food on the table, clean clothes on their children, and still set aside enough money for a better future. The clarinet whose notes were so surprisingly well played seemed both out of place and at once symbolic of what the residents could achieve given the opportunity. Music was the boy's escape, and for all I knew might one day be the key to his achieving a better life. At that moment there was no way to know.

I stood listening for a few minutes, absorbing the music. I did not think of who the boy was, how he came to have the clarinet, what brought him to the rooftop for his practice session, or what his plans might be for the future. I just listened, recognizing myself as one element of a tableau comprised of the young musician, myself as an audience of one, and the seemingly empty buildings serving as an outdoor concert shell.

I listened and then I moved on.

Earning One's Chops One Note at a Time:

Five decades passed. I married, became a father, and lived with my family on the near west side of Cleveland. I was still walking; still looking at and listening to parts of the city others seemed to overlook or ignore. Among them was the Cleveland Metropolitan Housing Authority's Riverfront Apartment Building on West 25th Street approximately half way between Detroit and Lorain. Or to be more specific, the RTA Bus Stop directly in front of the building.

This time the music was from a saxophone, not a clarinet. This time the musician was a somewhat weathered, one-legged man near to my own age. He sat with his prosthesis strap open, the artificial leg removed and leaning against the bench on which he sat. An instrument case was by his feet and sheet music was on his lap as he worked the fingering and timing for a Charlie Parker song he was trying to master.

The saxophone player lived in the Riverview, surviving on Social Security Disability payments and money people sometimes tossed in his case when he played downtown during a lunch hour or before a Cleveland Browns football game. He had loved the saxophone since he was in elementary school, loved jazz the first time he heard it, and delighted in reading about the life and work of various musicians. However, learning to play the saxophone was an effort made late in life, and because he wasn't a panhandler, never asking anyone for money, each time someone tipped him for his song, it was validation that his daily practice sessions were again paying off, that he had effectively added yet another number to his repertoire.

The result of the effort was music infused with love but not

16

with skill. He practiced every day in his small apartment, sometimes arising in the middle of the night for an extra practice session that would continue until a complaining neighbor sent him again out to the bus stop. Rain, snow, heat and cold did not matter. And in a bit of irony, through marriage he became a relative of The Sax Man.

Chapter Three

Meet the Sax Man

I may not even know the song,
but if I hear it in my head, I can play it.

The Sax Man stands in front of the stately theaters lining Cleveland's Playhouse Square, staring into a past whose sights, sounds, and sensual pleasures are performing on the stages of memory. He puts the horn to his lips, and in his mind's eye there is once again an audience of tens of thousands seated in the stands and on the playing field of the Kansas City Royals Stadium. The present could be any time, any day, any Broadway show passing through the city of Cleveland. Memory's stage is locked in 1975, the time of the Kool Jazz Festival, an invitation event for which only the nation's finest Jazz, Pop, and R&B singers and musicians are considered for performing.

The Sax Man is suddenly lost in a mind meld of past and

present. He hears his cue and takes a step forward. It is 1975 and he moves in front of the other musicians to start his solo. It is the present, a weekend matinee in Cleveland's Palace Theater and he moves in front of the theater goers being unloaded from cars and taxis.

It is 1975 and zoom lens-equipped television cameras focus on his hands, fingers flying on the keys of his saxophone, the image transferred to a mammoth television screen at one side of the playing field. It is the present and both teenagers and adults take out their cell phone cameras, flashes illuminating the Sax Man and the passers-by putting money in his case.

It is 1975 and the Sax Man is in Kansas as one of the back-up musicians for the singing group Sly, Slick, and Wicked whose successful recording for People/ Polydor Records, James Brown's label, has sent the trio on a heady trip, first to appear on *Soul Train*, the longest running television music show in history, and ultimately, after John "Sly" Wilson teaches the Sax Man and other talented back-up musicians the music and choreography for their performance, to the invitation only 1975 Kool Jazz Festival.

The Sax Man knew that the prestige of performing at such a festival was often the high point of a musician's career, a validation of his or her years of practice, performances, and recording success. The Sax Man also knew there were those who questioned his presence. He was just 22 years old and had only owned a saxophone since he was in Rawlings Junior High where his first band, The Dynamics, was noted for its earliest repertoire—two different songs they had to repeat over and over to if they were asked to perform for more than 7 or 8 minutes. He was invited to play his horn behind Sly, Slick & Wicked, a Cleveland trio that would eventually achieve national success

19

and international acclaim. John Wilson, the de facto leader of the trio, hired the Sax Man on the word of a friend who, like Wilson, had never heard the Sax Man play.

The Sax Man knew that many of the musicians performing at the Jazz Festival would be dismissive if they thought he hadn't earned his "chops." The Jazz Festival was the most meaningful stop on the Sax Man's first tour as a professional musician. He hoped to extend the work for so long as possible before a better saxophone player auditioned for the trio and was hired immediately. No one had talked of replacing him. No one was aware of his personal failings. They hired him without knowing him and worked with him when they saw the explosive talent the Sax Man would never see in himself. And so he continued to avoid revealing the secret that would haunt his life for forty years. The Sax Man was dyslexic.

The Sax Man could not comprehend books. He could not comprehend newspapers. He could not comprehend music printed on a page. He learned his instrument by ear and by watching the fingering other saxophone players used when they were mastering whatever music they were all to be playing.

The Sax Man told no one of his disability, in large part because the Cleveland Public School tutors and special education teachers who understood the condition, who could have explained that dyslexia did *not* mean he was stupid, chose to pass him from grade to grade without comment. They may have thought they were doing him a favor when they gave him a diploma despite his lack of written language skills. They may have thought the lanky black kid was hopeless so why send him to programs for dyslexic adults even though educators such as those with the Montessori system had, for decades, been helping children and adults overcome the problem.

Whatever the motivation of those who should have done more for the Sax Man, he came to what he felt was the only possible conclusion. He was too dumb to read, too dumb to write, too dumb to be a professional musician. He might get a gig here and there. He had lucked into being hired by John Wilson to play behind Sly, Slick, & Wicked, never realizing that when they finally heard him play, they thought he might eventually be among the greatest saxophone players of his generation. Instead, he was certain that when the others realized he couldn't read music, couldn't read at all, that he was slower than others in mastering the horn lines for the music they played, he would be fired. A more talented horn player, someone who could read a score or pick-up on the instrumentals the first time through instead of needing seemingly endless time listening to his part, then working to play what he heard, would take his place on stage. He was certain he would be left with nothing but the love of an instrument he never realized he had mastered in his own unique way.

[In discussing his limitations, Maurice explained that he had learned to read aloud with no obvious problems with phrasing and pronunciation. Retention of the material he was reading was something else. He was a little like students who have mastered pronunciation but not comprehension when first studying a foreign language, or singers learning a song in a different tongue. Their audience may think they are fluent in the previously unfamiliar tongue but the reality is that they have little or no comprehension of what they are correctly pronouncing.

Maurice did not sound as though he was having trouble, did not tell anyone he could not comprehend what he had just said, and was able to fool all those for whom he had to read.]

Chapter Four

The Youth in Pain

"My parents divorced when I was 8 years old. I remember him coming home from work and all that. He worked at Cleveland Metal Bed with mother's father. He was an upholsterer. Worked day and music at night. Then Post Office when Maurice a baby. Clerk typist. Fired for falling asleep on the job. He was playing with a group. 1967 Fourteen years old. Went to live with my father. Father always told me that when

"I got old enough I could come live with him. I was seven years old when I first asked.

"On the road a lot. Columbus based for just music. The group was the Lonny Wood Trio then went to The New Fools. He did comedy. They had a singer. Then him and Big John the drummer. Did a comedy routine with my father.

"I remember going to the union on weekends with him. He

went to the union [Musicians Union] a lot.

"I stayed with my father about six months. Then he started traveling and I went home. Went to Champion Junior High School in Columbus. Couldn't get into a band. Lost almost a year. My father bought me some drums, conga drums, and I played them at the neighborhood center. I was in a show. And then my father had me go down to a club with him, a place called the Cadillac Club. Saturdays I would go down with them and play on the stage. I was fourteen years old. He would take me to the clubs with him at night. He was taking me to clubs when I was 10 or 11 years old, take me to the club when he was playing.

"I had all the freedom in the world, man. I couldn't do some of the stuff if I was with my mother. I couldn't go out and play with the band and smoke cigarettes and all that kind of stuff. I thought I was cool. I was doing all that stuff. You know, having my own bedroom and hearing the music play all night. The record player playing and don't nobody saying nothing. I had my little record player and my transistor radio. Had 8 track tapes.

"I remember everyone giving me standing ovations. They gave me a lot of solos. I used to get a lot of applause when I played the congas.

Chapter Five

The Story of Blind Eddie

There were two major influences in what would become the professional life of Maurice Reedus, Jr. One was John Wilson, a singer, writer, producer and arranger who founded the trio *Sly, Slick & Wicked*, then hired Maurice to be one of the group's back-up musicians. And the other was a young man of similar age to Reedus and Wilson, a conga player who was known as Blind Eddie Smoot.

Eddie Smoot provides a way

Eddie Smoot had come of age in the world of music opportunities in Cleveland's ghetto areas. He would go from club to club, booking gigs and gradually gaining a mostly adult following that seemed to belie his age. His musicianship was highly respected and it was believed that he would eventually leave Cleveland and perform nationally. Then came the accident. It would change not only his life but also the lives of numerous musically inclined boys including the young Maurice Reedus who, until he began learning from Blind Eddie, had shown little interest in music except as it might make him look as "cool" as his father. The boys who worked with and learned from Eddie were uncertain about what caused his accident. What is known is that the flamboyant performer decided to add flash to the appearance of his congas. To this end he bought paint supplies and created a design to reproduce on his drums.

Perhaps the size of the congas made it awkward to both hold and paint them. Or the project might have been too difficult for one person to handle. A third possibility was he simply became careless. All that is certain is that some of the chemicals splashed into Eddie Smoot's eyes. By the time medical help arrived it was too late to save his sight.

The story of the blind conga player is remarkable for Smoot's lack of bitterness. He still played the congas after the accident, yet realizing that there would be limitations to greater success, he decided to teach other youths what he knew about the drums, changing their lives through the music he loved.

Performing became secondary to teaching others what he knew, and towards this end he created The Courageous Young Men.

. . .

The Courageous Young Men were boys who lived in the Garden Valley Estates and surrounding low income neighbor-

25

hood. Their days were often spent in the midst of the temptations of the streets—petty thievery, shoplifting, drugs, gang activity and the like. Most boys had a friend or family member who had been arrested at one time or another. That was why Smoot chose the location to form his own "gang" of boys who loved music, who were fascinated by the congas that Eddie still played, and were willing to devote the time to practicing needed to truly succeed. In addition, because they were chosen from the immediate area, they could walk to and from school together. They could go together for practice sessions. They did not have to worry about someone taking advantage of them because they were on the streets alone. Their numbers assured they could avoid problems with neighborhood trouble makers.

Blind Eddie did not just hang out at the Garden Valley Neighborhood Center where most of the practice sessions were held. He inserted himself into every aspect of the lives of the boys who were accepted into his conga band. Guided by his friend, Smoot visited the homes of each of the boys. He talked with the parents. He talked with siblings and any extended family. He insisted the Courageous Young Men do their homework, behave at home, at school, and when playing outdoors. He became part mentor, part father figure, and part inspiration at the same time he taught them the mastery of the instrument on which he was so skilled.

. . .

"We thought [performing] was cool because the other kids wasn't doing what we was doing. All my friends... We was going out and doing the shows. We had to sit together, eat together... He'd tell us how much food to get when we were in some community center or little private parties. Don't nobody put cookies in their pockets. And he had people watching us so we used to get caught all the time trying to sneak stuff. We were chaperoned but we tried to sneak. Cookies, man, we was going to eat them. Candy... We tried to put it in our pockets. And gentlemen... We had to sneak to do a lot of stuff around our director. We'd sit together and we'd everybody go eat. It was like everybody take two cookies apiece and that's it. And no one go up for seconds.

"I'm glad he did it that way, now. But we would crumble up the cookies and put them in our pockets so no one could see the shape. Just reach in our hands and put cookies in our mouths. Weren't nobody looking. Like back in the little dressing room they had us in, though we got caught a couple of times. Eddie... He's a blind man catching us. I couldn't believe that. We got caught doing a whole lot of stuff. He disciplined us well. He was our teacher. If we got in trouble at home he'd get on us. He'd find stuff out. At school he'd find stuff out. We had to be in at certain times because we was going to school. Some of us were in elementary school so we couldn't stay out late. We would be in 8:30 or 9 o'clock to get up in the morning at 7 o'clock for school. Plus there was homework and chores around the house.

"We tried to find our own time. We'd be out playing together and Eddie would send kids to find us. "We'd be down in the dump playing by the Dan-Dee Potato Chip factory. We had a Tarzan swing tied to a tree we used to swing on."

. . .

27

[I was] 11 years old. I was living in Garden Valley. This was 1964 and they had a Garden Valley neighborhood house for all the kids in the neighborhood. And there was a guy auditioning young boys to put a musical group together. There were 25 little boys and out of 25 little boys, he wanted six. Out of 25 boys, I was one of them.

The name of our group was Eddie Smoot and the Courageous Young Men (CY boys). As we played the music, he would stand in front of us and direct us. This was a blind man directing us. It was three conga players, two guys on maracas, and we had a bongo player. We did all the Motown songs, the songs that were out, but we did it all on drums. There were no guitars, no horns, no nothing, just the conga drums.

We'd learn any song we wanted, and we put beats in every song that we did. We had one song called I'm Going Back To School. I'm going back... going back to school. Last words of the whole song were "Play it cool, stay in school."

[Eddie] got on us if he heard we were getting into trouble in school. We'd get punished by him if he heard about us acting up over anything. This man was so disciplined, he used to make us so mad at him. We figured he couldn't see so we could do shit. We used to do all kinds of stuff. We used to do stuff, try to sneak stuff.

We figured that Mickey, the guy who used to be our chaperone, was telling him, which he probably did. But a lot of times he wasn't around, and this man (Eddie) would be like walking to his house and finding his clothes and shining his shoes and work on his car. He was like a big brother or father to us. We never missed a rehearsal. We was like little boys. We got into all kinds of mischief, but we never missed a rehearsal, and if we did miss a rehearsal, he would send guys looking for us.

Eddie would say, "Get over here right now!" and then you'd be scared to go. He'd make us stand on one leg in the corner and have somebody watch us. Or have us doing work around the house. We

28

learned a lot. For me being with him when I was 11 or 12 years old, and I left him when I was 17 years old, I didn't know how I was going to do it. How could we just leave him? But he wanted us to go on. He really started everyone's career. Out of all the guys that are in to music in the group, only two of us are still playing into music full time. Johnny Britt, and he's in California. He was the musical director for one of the Temptations' tour. Youngest one of all of us. He was like the baby of the group. When I was 15, Johnny Britt was probably 11 or 12. I was five years older than Johnny. And I always wanted to play the saxophone, but during that time, when I was a kid, I was like too little. And into the bongo drums. Eddie Smoot used to supply us with the drums. All the drums we played with were his drums, but we used to take them home and play with them and have rehearsal.

We started doing the talent shows in the neighborhood. We did shows at the WHK Building which was downtown. We had write-up in the newspaper the Call & Post. We went on Gene Carroll. We did Upbeat. We were on channel 61. We did a lot of churches, parties. These little boys playing the conga drums and this man standing up in front directing them. Eddie Smoot gave all our money to our parents. We didn't know what it was. We didn't really care so long as we got candy and cookies back then. If we had a dollar in our pocket, we were rich. We were cool. Go to school with a dollar and a pocket full of candy...

In the sixth grade, when I went from elementary school to Rawlings Junior High School, the first thing I wanted to do was get in the band and learn how to play the saxophone. Mr. Foster was my first band teacher. He used to be my mother's gym teacher when she was in school.

Me and my sister started us on clarinet the first year. And the second year I went to the baritone sax. I had the biggest horn in the

29

whole band. The baritone saxophone. I'm little. I was maybe five feet tall.

When you first join the band, the teacher's teaching everyone at the same time. He can't focus on everybody. But if an individual needs help, you raise your hand and he comes help you, but my main problem was reading the notes. For some reason I couldn't just read those dots. I'd sit there like everybody else. I had a problem with learning which back in those days my mother didn't know what to do. Back in the fifties, my mother was pregnant with me and the doctor, he was supposed to cut her and pull me out. They fired the doctor, too, because my mother—my foot was stuck up in her and they pulled me out feet first. Back then, when I went to school, I should have been going to one of those special schools. People were saying I wasn't paying attention. I didn't know. I was a perfect reader. I used to love to stand up in front of the class and read but I didn't understand what I was reading.

I used to get on punishment, whuppings [sic]... because all the teachers said, "Well, he's not paying attention and I was the clown. They said I was trying to get attention because I wanted to be like everyone else. But I couldn't. I couldn't understand it. I couldn't even count on my fingers.

As I got older, I felt like I was really stupid. Man, I was terrible at school. Back then they passed me because of age. The teachers liked me so they went ahead and passed me. In high school it got even weirder. I was in Warrensville Heights High School [instead of one offering special education], an academic high school [college prep]. I couldn't believe it. [They had] humanities and all that. Humanities? What is this?

I knew all the Beetles' songs. I mean, I learned them all word by word because I loved the Beetles' songs. And I know all the cartoon songs. Yogi Bear and that. I may not even know the song, but if I hear it in my head, I can play it.

. . .

Reedus might have been in awe of his father but for reasons that have never been clear, he rarely chose to ask the older man for guidance either as a sax player or as a musician seeking gigs both in Cleveland and out of town.

Maurice, Sr. traveled the world and was a Grammy winning recording artist. Maurice, Jr. seemed more concerned with validation from his father for his choice of what proved to be an eccentric professional career path in and out of clubs, with bands and alone, and for earning the bulk of his income from performing on the streets.

The Sax Man still talks frequently of his late father, a man he adored. However, it is not his father's Grammy winning musicianship of which he speaks. Rather it is the fact, in the son's mind, that his father had been the epitome of "cool." How the older man dressed, both for the stage and for casual wear, how he held himself when talking with fans and when performing before an audience, even the saxophone arrangements he played, all represented to the younger Reedus his idea of the highest achievement of a musician's art. What the Sax Man doesn't mention is having conversations with his father about music theory, playing styles, or even tricks of a comedian's trade since both men long ago added a comedy segment to almost every show of which they were a part.

Musicians who have known both men praise the elder Reedus for his willingness to share what he knew about jazz, blues, and performing in general. By contrast, some have complained that the Sax Man, when asked the same questions his father so freely answered, will not respond. He is too busy, they claim he says, resenting his refusal to pass his knowledge to the next generation. However, whether this is because the Sax Man is insecure about the possibility that someone he helps will take gigs from him or because he does not see himself as deserving of such respect is not known.

Whatever their differences, the Sax Man's father did not criticize the path his son chose for himself when he walked away from full time band work and began performing primarily on the street. Rather than being disappointed in his son's choice, he always accepted his son's decisions about a career no matter how eccentric. He loved his son for who he was.

. . .

"I'd be in the audience and the band's on stage. They're getting ready to start a song. They start playing a song and I'm walking around the club. I'm booing them off the stage. The band was doing different songs. Whatever they would play, it looked like they were starting their show. I would walk around booing them. Boo! Boo! Boo! Boo! And one of the guys in the band would say, "Man, what's wrong with you?"

"Ain't nothing wrong with me. What's wrong with you?"

He'd say, "Ladies and gentlemen, you have to excuse that guy out there. I think he's drunk or something."

I'd say, "Drunk? I ain't drunk! You ugly!"

"You drunk!"

"You ugly"

"You drunk!"

And I'd say, "Yeah, but in the morning I'll be sober, but you'll still ugly.

Then he'd say, "Man, you must think you're bad or some-thing."

I'd say, "Damn right. I'm so bad I can walk a barbed wire fence with two bearcats eating my arms. I've got a graveyard disposition and I don't mind dying."

Then he'd say, "You don't mess with me. You don't mess with me."

"I'll knock you down so low, you'll have to reach up to tie your shoes."

"Well, if you think you can entertain the people..."

So I said to them, "First of all, tell me what's in back of the stage."

What do you mean, "What's in back of the stage?"

Just what I said. What's in back of the stage? "Ain't nothing in back of the stage.

Then I would say, "I know. Ain't nothing in front of it either."

By then everybody would be laughing and he'd say, "Well, if you think you're so good, and you can entertain the people, why don't you come up and sing a song"

"Yeah, I'll come up and sing a song. And I come over and say, 'This is a number by the Ex-Lax brothers. And this song is called *Doo-Doo*. And I sing Doo doo doo doo doo doo. People start laughing and I go into my routine.

. . .

Joe Siebert: "You talk about these people and how eccentric they are, but Maurice, he's just one of them who never made it to the big time, but he's still like that eccentric...he's like the guy...A cool dude, but he's strange. "It's sad when you see some-

33

one so talented be a slave to certain elements of their life. I've seen Maurice now, enough, to kind of get an idea of what's really there. The drug habit... I think it's been killing him a long time."

. . .

Maurice Reedus, Jr.: Leo's Casino. They changed the name to the Club Kabana 1971 or 1972 we [Foreign Blue] opened for the Staple Singers. Then we opened for Gladys Knight and the *Pips*. That's with the Foreign Blue, the first band I really started with.

We just was on the show and opened up for a couple of acts. They liked the group. We went there and auditioned and then they hired us. In the afternoon. Set up on the stage. And then I did another job in another place, and the sheriff owned the East Town Motor Lodge on Euclid. They had nothing but top name entertainment there a couple of times." Leo's was the second club where Maurice did his comedy routine.

He auditioned for the owner and maybe a couple of bar maids. When we went to Leo's we didn't audition, went in and talked about the band. Showed him pictures. Heard him for the first time when warming up. "Previous Sir Rah House, East Town, Club Kabana, Also Brougham Lounge 105th and Euclid. Club 106—previously called the Circle Ballroom. O'Neil's Show bar—Bob O'Neil. Back in the 60s and 70s they was hustlers. They always had a piece of the action. Real suave, debonair

"They dressed sharp. They always wore really sharp suits. Had their hair in the process—the waves in the hair. Drove big cars. Drove Cadillacs. They just had money. That movie [the movie] *Superfly* was out. Names on license plates, flaps over the tires. Eli Tell-A-Lie comedian who was MC at the Brougham Lounge.

"I felt kind of intimidated a little bit because I feel he [Eli] was more of a comedian than me. I was wondering would I be funny to him? Would he respect me as a comedian? He was older than I was. His jokes was all right but he just had a different style of telling jokes. And I had just started telling my jokes, you know. But he liked me. He thought it was funny."

During an extended trip to California Maurice decided to go to some of the comedy clubs that had open mike nights early in the week. The pressure on the comics was less that night, though the expectations were greater. The house was small, most of the audience either new comics trying to learn stage presence while playing off the club's patrons or experienced comics trying new material on the smallest audience they could find. Top performers like Johnny Carson who "owned" late night television as long time host of the Tonight Show would come late on an open mike night.

There was also the opportunity for new comics to be heard and booked for television and nightclub appearances. Someone who was unusually effective in the comedy club environment but just entering show business might be offered a job by the club owner. He or she would become the house comic, the master of ceremonies who would introduce acts, play off the performers who bombed and didn't have the sense to leave the stage, and do jokes between acts. There was no greater compliment short of a television booker handing the comic a multi-week contract to appear on one or another variety shows.

"I did the Comedy Club on Sunset Boulevard. Every comedian in the world played the Comedy Club. Los Angeles. Friday night. The Laff Stop. The night you could go up and sign the list to perform a set of five or ten minutes. (Comedy Club) I was the last for the night.

"Laff Stop in Encino called me and wanted me to come back there. Hired me to do Comedy Store. They taped everyone. Had me on video." "The 70s was the best era. I wish I could tell jokes again. I stayed with my brother in San Bernadino. We were still in LA, in Hollywood. I called the Comedy Store to find out what night they had comedy."

Scared to go in the club alone, Maurice convinced a friend and fellow musician, Ghani Harris, to come with him.

Ghani was not enthusiastic. Maurice was unknown, familiar professionally as a musician, not a comic. He had never performed before such an important audience, and being the last act of the night, Ghani assumed, probably rightfully, that the last act would be the one on which the audience walked out. And at first that assessment seemed the correct one.

"People were walking out the door, and when they announced 'Maurice Reedus from Cleveland, Ohio.' Ghani said everybody made a U-turn because they knew Arsenio Hall was from Cleveland, Ohio during that time. So I heard some people in the audience say, 'We hope you're not going to sell out like Arsenio Hall.' Several people in the audience said that to me. I guess he did whatever he had to do, to change his material to get a laugh. To me, he wasn't all that funny. He did clean and it wasn't really funny. My sister went to school with him. I knew him from Warrensville Heights High School. I knew him before he got big. He used to be a magician they say when he was in high school. He used to do little tricks and stuff.

"Each time I was on the stage I was imitating my father. My father had never been in the Comedy Store. I'm telling my father's jokes. You have to remember the expressions he used to make on your face. In the comedy club they had this great big light and you can't really see. That's what I liked about it. People can see you but you can't really see them. So I can just do my thing and ain't nobody looking.

"Sometimes I'll say, 'Damn, where you all at?' But I was for real. I can't see none of you people. Talk about a bright light. Damn. I wonder if this is the same light you see when you die?'

"Everybody started laughing. I'm telling the truth. I really can't see you people. I'm seeing the bright light, though. They laughed on that for a minute. I said, y'all laughing but I'm serious.

"Then I said, speaking of light, do you all know the difference between a light sleeper and a hard sleeper?

"Everybody said no.

"A light sleeper sleeps with the light on. And then they really started laughing. My father did that joke. Then you got to pause. A light sleeper sleeps with the light on. A hard sleeper sleeps with a hard on.

"I would always end my show, I would say, before my last joke and went off the stage. I would make a toast. 'Before I leave you here tonight, I want to make a toast: Here's to women, creature divine, she blossoms every month and bares every nine. The only thing on this side of Hell that can get goodies from the nut without cracking the shell.'

"Then I'd be walking off the stage and they'd be cracking up. Or I'd say, "Confucius was a wise man. Confucius say, 'Impossible for man to rape woman. Woman run much faster with dress up than man with pants down.'

"I got that one from my father, too. And then I'd say something like, 'Here's a toast to all the ugly people in the world. See, this way I have more friends.' I leave them with something I know they're going to laugh at as I walk off the stage.

"Sometimes I'd say, 'I'll see you all later. I'm gone unless you're going to pay me some more money.' Stuff like that.

"I did about 20 or 25 minutes at the Comedy Store. I was the last comedian so I went long. And when I got off the stage everybody was patting me on the back. All the other comedians. They said I should start coming around to the workshop. People like you. It was right around the time that Redd Foxx passed away and wasn't nobody doing Redd Foxx material. They said I'm the first comedian ever coming in that club doing his (Foxx) material. It was original the way you did it. I guess nobody ever tried to mess with Redd Foxx stuff.

"He did X rated jokes."

Maurice had to use what amounted to family oriented material—either avoided saying jokes that would upset parents who took their children to an early show or making certain that if they heard some of the material, they wouldn't understand it. And so...

. . .

"Ladies and gentlemen, it's really nice to appear here tonight. It really is nice to appear anywhere tonight. My landlord told me that if I wasn't going to appear here, I would disappear from there.

"It's nice to be looking down into some of your faces this evening. Your faces need some looking into. There's a bunch of ugly people here tonight. You don't have to believe me. Just look into the face next to you. "And then I say, you really got to see my old lady to believe in Halloween. It's Halloween time, but when I first met my old lady, I thought she had a mask on. I ain't lying. She's just ugly for no particular reason. I mean she's so ugly her hair's so short, you can smell her brain. She's so cross eyed, when she cries, the tears run down her back. They asked me, 'Maurice, would you take her for better or for worse?'

"I said, hell. I think I can do better. I can't do no worse.

"I would take my wife everywhere I go just to keep from kissing her goodbye.

"And then I would say, I want to make a toast. You know when most entertainers come out on stage, they dedicate the show to all the lovely people in the house. Well, I think that's wrong to keep out the ugly people. I dedicate my show to all the ugly people. That way I have more friends.

"And then I would say, 'I was talking to my wife this morning, and I said, Baby, what are you doing?

"She said, 'I'm going downtown to buy me a brassiere.' "I said, 'But you ain't got shit to put in it.'

She looked at me and said, "Hell, you wear shorts..."

Have you ever been walking through the park in the dark? Down in the bushes? Alone? Naked in the park. You all get the plot.

"Hey baby, I wish I had a flashlight so I could see what I'm doing.' "Hell, yeah, I wish you had a flashlight, too, because you've been eating grass for fifteen minutes."

"My father could sit down and do a whole show for you just sitting down. I would try to imitate him. A lot of material. But if I'm on a stage in front of a lot of people, it just comes to me. It's forced to come to me.

"And then after the last show I would say, 'Well, if I offended anyone in the course of my show, I would like to tell you from deep down far in my heart, that I don't give a shit."

Then I would walk off stage. They would be laughing or whatever. And then I would run back stage. The band would still be on stage. They'd go into a song. I'd take off my overalls and come back on the stage and join the band, and introduce the Foreign Blue. This was before Sly, Slick & Wicked. The only difference was with Foreign Blue I didn't introduce the foreign blue. They would already be on stage. I'd just join the band in the middle of a song. But with Sly, Slick & Wicked I would re-join the band. We would finish the song and then I'd introduce Sly, Slick, & Wicked.

"Ladies and Gentlemen, are you ready for show time? Are you ready for show time? I'd like to know, are you ready for show time? I would like to introduce to the stage, Paramount Recording artists. And then I would say, 'Who brought to you their hit record *Surely, Stay My Love*. Ladies and gentlemen, can we bring to the stage. How about a nice round of applause for Cleveland's own, New York recording artists—SLY, SLICK, AND WICKED!

We'd do the musical intro and then they'd run out on stage. And that's how the show started.

But I would have a different crowd of people up. They'd be screaming and hollering because they'd be waiting up all night for Sly, Slick, and Wicked. They got posters all around town about Sly, Slick & Wicked. They bought the record. They'd been listening to the radio station and all that.

Sometimes I would come out and the first part of my routine I would say, "Shut up! Shut up!" Shut up, everybody!" and everybody would get quiet. Then I'd say, "Ain't going to be no talking while I'm interrupting!" That was one approach. After that, I would say, "Good evening, ladies and gentlemen...and you others. You know before I walked into the club tonight, I seen two gay people out front and they were out there arguing, and I would listen to them. And one of the gay people said, "I'm not going in there." And the other one said, "Why not?"

"Because I'm pregnant and they'll laugh at me."

"How in the hell did you get pregnant?"

"I don't know. I ain't got eyes in the back of my head."

"I never knew what I was going to say when I got started. Back then I had stuff written down until I learned my routine. I'd just go into whatever. I might go into ugly people or I'd talk about Benjamin Franklin.

I'd say, "When white people go home they tell black stories. I hear the gentle voices calling (sung) old black Joe.

"When we go home, we tell white stories. We all know Benjamin Franklin was a queer. Why else would he be outside in chilled knickers, flying a kite in pigtails, waiting on a charge? "Strike it, Lightning! Lightning did it! Hell, lightning was colored. Ain't never seen no white lightning before."

"I'd tell some military jokes. I backed up so far in one battle, I ran into a general. The general said, "Private, why are you running?" I said, "General, I'm running because I cannot fly."

I never did no specific comedy show. They were coming for whoever the main act was. I was like an opening act. I would do my act before the main show.

They had some people who would heckle me. I would embarrass them. People would say, "Get off the stage. You ain't funny. And I would say something like, "I don't come on your job and take away your mop and broom away from you. Stuff like that.

Pantomines jerking at his crotch and says, "I would shut you up permanently but my zipper's stuck." Some people would really get upset at that. They'd get mad and want to beat me up."

And then I would say something like, "Don't get offended. I'm only serious."

"Some people would get offended, especially people sitting in the front. Somebody sitting right up front saying something to me... A lot of times I had to get escorted out of the club. They'd be waiting for me to come out. And the security or the police they'd walk me out, make sure I got out okay. Because some people they had to put out of the club for interrupting the show. It happened once at the Checkmate at Shaker Square. And it happened one night up at the Sir Rah House. And it happened at this other club called the Funky Broadway at 131st and Broadway. The Kinsman Grille on 128th and Kinsman. But I never got a chance to tell no jokes with a white audience.

"The first mixed audience that I told jokes at was in Encino, California. They had the Laff Stop. That was the first mixed race audience I ever told jokes at, and that was in 1981. It was a comedy club John took me to. It was an open mike night. I used to go there like every other week, me and John, and I always wanted to do my comedy routine.

. . .

Maurice, Sr., may have accepted his son's choices but other musicians frequently have not. His critics consider the Sax Man to be lazy. They say he wants to be a great sax player but he doesn't want to do the intense amount of practicing needed to get there. They often hold his choice of street theater in disdain and wonder how many passers-by pay attention to what he considers almost a calling.

Certainly the Sax Man's musicianship is backed, not by instrumentalists of similar caliber but by the musical cacophony created by squealing car brakes, raucous truck horns, mindless cell phone chatter, and, as night settles in on the city, the rising voices of arguing couples headed for either a break-up in their relationship or a resolution leading to late night make-up sex.

The Sax Man treats his sidewalk stage with the same enthusiasm as if he was working the Palace Theater directly behind where he stands on Playhouse Square. His horn's mouthpiece pressed to his lips, he bobs and weaves with his instrument as though it had magical properties, the notes pouring forth a physical presence capable of encompassing each man, woman, and child, holding them long enough for them to hear a phrase or two before releasing them to enter the show, the sporting event, the restaurant. Even those who consider him a nuisance, who try to ignore his performance, slow their steps, pause in their journey, and just for an instant are transported to a quieter time, a gentler place, a happier moment. It is a performer's art, and in the case of the Sax Man, it can be traced back five decades to when the then adolescent fledgling musician was working with Eddie Smoot.

. . .

The Sax Man's routine takes him among the business and entertainment sections of downtown Cleveland. Between midday lunch time and the closing of the bars, music, and comedy clubs, an estimated 130,000 men and women will hear the Sax Man in any given week. Some are rushing to the opening curtain of a touring Broadway show. Some are lingering over a late night meal. Some are buying groceries and wine from Constantino's Market in preparation for a seductive evening with a current or hoped-for lover. Still others, the ones most people avoid, are using cardboard cartons, large pieces of plastic found in area Dumpsters, blankets from one of the churches' homeless outreach programs, and the heat from a steam grate close to the doorway of an unrented office to create a makeshift bedroom. And from that transient "hotel" they are likely to take a last drag on a cigarette, a last swig of what had been a pint of Thunderbird Wine, then close their eyes and let the music of the Sax Man drift over them, bringing them peace for another night.

. . .

Sanctified music, school bands, talent shows, and the projects

Cleveland in the 1950s and 1960s was no different from other cities with large concentrations of blacks who found acceptance, respect, purpose, and sometimes conflicts of theology and leadership within the various churches.

The churches often held the same opportunities for Blacks facing limited chances in the community at large that had once been available to European immigrants through settlement houses and neighborhood centers. Many churches serving low income and black areas had programs that both taught children to play musical instruments and gave them a chance to show their newly acquired skills to an avid, encouraging congregation. The opportunities when participating in one or another of the churches often included adult education, after school tutoring for children (usually accompanied by a treat prepared in the church kitchen by some of the mothers or grandmothers), Bible study, leadership instruction and music education—both instruments and voice – among other options.

The church programs also gave participating members of the congregation a respect they often lacked on the streets of Cleveland where a Black man could be invisible to white passers-by. ("They all look alike to me," was a familiar comment when a white man was asked to describe a Black man.). In the black church a man was recognized as a unique human being.

The Reedus family was not connected with a church music program. The young Maurice played in bands with boys who had experienced their first audiences on Sunday mornings. But the Sax Man's earliest training was something quite different. It took place in the Garden Valley Estates, the sprawling public housing project of 650 units. The families were a mix of those who would need long term housing and those who were using it as interim living quarters. Almost everyone had been displaced by Urban Renewal projects that purchased their previous living quarters directly or acquired them through eminent domain. What proved more important for a handful of children who made the move with their parents was the community center. This was a building available for education and recreation. The elderly might come together to play cards or checkers, to knit or to talk. There was a place to play basketball, but more important for the future Sax Man, there was a place to learn the congas.

. . .

"My first chance to be a performer came when I was 11-years-old and living in Garden Valley. This was 1964 and they had a Garden Valley neighborhood house for all the kids in the neighborhood. And there was a guy auditioning young boys to put a musical group together. There were 25 little boys and out of 25 little boys, he wanted six. Out of 25 boys, I was one of them.

"The name of our group was Eddie Smoot and the Courageous Young Men (CY boys). As we played the music, he would stand in front of us and direct us. This was a blind man directing us. It was three conga players, two guys on maracas, and we had a bongo player. We did all the Motown songs, the songs that were out, but we did it all on drums. There were no guitars, no horns, no nothing, just the conga drums.

"We'd learn any song we wanted, and we put beats in every song that we did. We had one song called *I'm Going Back to School*. I'm going back... going back to school. Last words of the whole song were 'Play it cool, stay in school.'

"He got on us if he heard we were getting into trouble in school. We'd get punished by him if he heard about us acting up over anything. This man was so disciplined, he used to make us so mad at him. We figured he couldn't see so we could do shit. We used to do all kinds of stuff. We used to do stuff, try to sneak stuff.

"We figured that Mickey, the guy who used to be our chaperone, was telling him, which he probably did. But a lot of times he wasn't around, and this man (Eddie) would be like walking to his house and finding his clothes and shining his shoes and work on his car. He was like a big brother or father to us. We never missed a rehearsal. We was like little boys. We got into all kinds of mischief, but we never missed a rehearsal, and if we did miss a rehearsal, he would send guys looking for us.

"Eddie would say, 'Get over here right now!' and then you'd be scared to go. He'd make us stand on one leg in the corner and have somebody watch us. Or have us doing work around the house. We learned a lot. For me being with him when I was 11 or 12 years old, and I left him when I was 17 years old, I didn't know how I was going to do it. How could we just leave him? But he wanted us to go on. He really started everyone's career. Out of all the guys that are in to music in the group, only two of us are still playing into music full time. Johnny Britt, and he's in California. He was the musical director for one of the Temptations' tour. Youngest one of all of us. He was like the baby of the group. When I was 15, Johnny Britt was probably 11 or 12. I was five years older than Johnny. And I always wanted to play the saxophone, but during that time, when I was a kid, I was like too little. And into the bongo drums. Eddie Smoot used to supply us with the drums. All the drums we played with were his drums, but we used to take them home and play with them and have rehearsal. "

. . .

The Courageous Young Men was more than just a group of kids playing a version of a school rhythm band. These were professional musicians, sometimes having performed for years and sometimes at the start of their careers

Johnny Britt was both unique and typical. Early in his life he, his mother and his sister lived with an aunt and uncle in a home that also served as his uncle's church, The House Of God, that later grew large enough to move into a building of its own.

Johnny became the choir's lead singer when only 4 years old, became one of the Courageous Young Men at 7, and became a self-taught trumpet player at 12. Eventually he attended Cleveland State University and the Versailles Conservatory of Music in Paris, and Governors State University in Chicago. He trained as a performer, arranger, and composer. He performed at the White House for then President Bill Clinton, and he performed at the Olympic Games in Atlanta. The groups with which he worked were among the most legendary in the country, including The Temptations for which he wrote songs and then worked as their music director.

The credits go on for several pages, and the fact that most of the Courageous Young Men had their own success tells more of about the inspiration of Blind Eddie Smoot than anything else. Even the Sax Man cannot be considered different from friends such as Johnny Britt. As eccentric as his life and career have been, Maurice Reedus remains daily pursuing the music career with which he is most comfortable, as eccentric as that often seems to his detractors.

. . .

"We started doing the talent shows in the neighborhood. We did shows at the WHK Building which was downtown. We had write up in the newspaper the Call & Post. We went on Gene Carroll. We did Upbeat. We were on channel 61. We did a lot of churches, parties. These little boys playing the conga drums and this man standing up in front directing them. Eddie Smoot gave all our money to our parents. We didn't know what it was. We didn't really care so long as we got candy and cookies back then. If we had a dollar in our pocket, we were rich. We were cool. Go to school with a dollar and a pocket full of candy.

"In the sixth grade, when I went from elementary school to Rawlings Junior High School, the first thing I wanted to do was get in the band and learn how to play the saxophone. Mr. Foster was my first band teacher. He used to be my mother's gym teacher when she was in school.

"As I got older, I felt like I was really stupid. Man, I was terrible at school. Back then they passed me because of age. The teachers liked me so they went ahead and passed me. In high school it got even weirder. I was in Warrensville Heights High School [instead of one offering special education], an academic high school [college prep]. I couldn't believe it. [They had] humanities and all that. Humanities? What is this?

"I knew all the Beetles' songs. I mean, I learned them all word by word because I loved the Beetles' songs. And I know all the cartoon songs. Yogi Bear and that.

"I may not even know the song, but if I hear it in my head, I can play it."

. . .

Maurice Reedus, Jr. may have worshiped his father and tried to imitate everything the older man did, but it was Blind Eddie Smoot who turned young Reedus into a professional musician. It was Smoot whose insistence on constant practice carried over into his eventual early mastery of the saxophone. And it was Smoot who taught the boys personal hygiene and the need to maintain a clean, well-dressed appearance. Finally, most important to the boys and least important to Smoot, he trained them to compete in the talent shows that were also an integral part of weekend television with programs such as local television's Gene Carroll Show and talent shows regularly held for students in the Cleveland Public School System.

The Courageous Young Men were entered in competitions at Rawlings Junior High where the majority went to school. The emphasis on music and the opportunities for professional play in nearby after-hours joints and weekend afternoon jam sessions meant that some of the singers, soloists, and bands were far more skilled than would be expected of students so young. They also had to audition for the teachers in charge so that by the time the competition was held, the quality of the performances was closer to that of college students than boys and girls not yet in high school.

Despite this advantage, the sense of competition was intense. The one overriding concern when young Reedus and the others rehearsed for the talent show—outplaying all the competition. He didn't realize that Smoot was adding what would become Reed's first comedy to the music performance.

. . .

The first gigs for Maurice were much the same as older musicians, including his father, described. Everyone earned their chops and learned to work together playing at the birthday parties of classmates and their siblings. They played for school dances known as canteens, events where most of the time the boys clustered on one side of the gym and the girls clustered on the other. Everybody looked across the floor, giggling, whispering comments, being too scared to actually ask someone to dance. Hormones might have started raging but they weren't ready to actually touch a member of the opposite sex. Instead, when they weren't talking about some special boy who didn't yet know girls existed, they would gather around the band, picking their favorites and flirting with the boys, all of whom were classmates, between sets.

Being in a band the teenagers liked playing for their canteens led to the band being hired for more sophisticated work. There were birthdays and special events, and in the summer this sometimes meant barbecues in the Kinsman and Garden Valley area where he lived. These summer backyard, neighborhood parties allowed the adults to talk, drink beer, and eat whatever had been slow cooked on the grill, while their older children danced to whichever among the latest popular songs the band had mastered.

Maurice and his friends felt they were finding success, not realizing that they were hired because they kept the teens at the parties occupied in ways that were not destructive. But even if the reason for their presence was not a reflection of their skills, Maurice and his friends were gaining in ability. And if Maurice could not play very well, the others would just play louder, drowning out his mistakes. What mattered to them was that they had become The Dynamics, a part of their first band, a rite of passage for a musician at least the equal of a first meaningful kiss or becoming a licensed driver.

"I remember it being really exciting. I remember trying to impress people and impress my friends. It was like a dream come true. I was actually playing with a band, the first band.

"We used to wear black pants, and what we knew as 'Hi-Boys'—white cotton shirts with big collars on them that we had starched. We went to a clothing store downtown at 9th

51

and Prospect by the Standard Theater where they showed what they called Triple-X rated movies. We used to get all our clothes down there. And across the street from there was Jack Epsteins' [ProspectMusic]." The latter was the store where professional musicians and musicians working to become professionals could buy quality instruments and accessories.

"I was in the Dynamics for the three years I went to Rawlings Junior High. I was still playing with Eddie Smoot and The Courageous Young Men," a fact that became difficult when Rawlings Junior High held a talent show for all the kids who were in bands, singers, dancers, or otherwise had a talent with which they wanted to compete. The Courageous Young Men and The Dynamics were in the show, Maurice effectively competing with himself on two different instruments.

"We [The Courageous Young Men] did talent shows the same day as the Dynamics did one. Smoot, wanting to set apart his boys so they would stand out, "had the idea of two of us in the band being dressed up as Batman and Robin. Since I was real tall, I wanted to be Batman but Eddie wanted us to look awkward so he had me dressed up as Robin, and I was pissed. A real short guy was Batman. We had these outfits on. I'm dressed up like Robin with these tights on. That was so embarrassing, but it was funny to the people.

"We came up [to perform] last, [to perform] and it was weird because I had to go back and put on those clothes, trying not to wear those tights, but I ended up putting them on anyway, and I was the most talked about guy around Rawlings.

"Back then I really didn't know I wanted to go into comedy," though he quickly liked the applause, the laughter, and the one-on-one relationship with the audience comedy made possible. Still, he saw himself as being a musician first.

Maurice, Sr. and Anita's divorce
Maurice, Sr. enters show business

The 1950s was a time when the elder Reedus first served in the military and then began a career as a musician and comedian. He was ready to travel anywhere and anytime in order to play whatever band needed him, whatever club wanted him. For his base, though, he chose Cleveland, and when the family became eligible for the Garden Valley housing, he helped with the relocation of his by-then ex-wife and children.

The divorce of the Sax Man's parents had been unpleasant for the young Maurice and his siblings, but in many ways the forced separation was not so hard on Maurice, Jr. His father had always been almost a mythic figure who seemed to move in and out of his life like a figure in a fairy tale who watched over him. The travels needed to obtain work meant that, if anything, the young Maurice would see his father almost as frequently as before, and it was still his father who was likely to be called by the school when Maurice deliberately acted up.

The move to Garden Valley helped Maurice in another, totally unexpected way. Neighborhood people often volunteered to work with the kids who lived in the project, participating in after school and weekend programs. And among those who reached out to the children was the young man who by then was known as Blind Eddie Smoot.

. . .

The relationship between Maurice, Jr. and his mother, Anita Reedus Taylor (she remarried, her new husband being the family connection to Kelvin Taylor), was much like that of an alcoholic and his/her enabler, a loved one who buys what the alcoholic must never have to make that person beholden and dependent.

Anita Reedus Taylor had been hurt by the necessity of a divorce from her musician husband. He was a handsome man, extremely intelligent, gifted as a musician, and a sophisticate from his travels to perform. He was also typical of the young men, eventually including his son, who are delighted with the seduction efforts of the women they meet on the road. They consider themselves faithful if they never have an affair in their home city. Beyond that, anything goes. The problem comes with their failing to consider the vows their spouses considered sacred wherever their musician husbands traveled.

The residual anger concerning the senior Maurice's actions leading to the divorce was palpable to an outsider. This writer first encountered it in an unexpected way. I wrote a cover story about Maurice, Jr., for the alternative weekly *Free Times*. It told of everything from how he learned music despite his dyslexia to his determination to be a traveling musician just like his father. He also told how his father was his role model for playing in bands.

The casual observer might note a couple of mentions of the elder Reedus and the publication included photos of the two men playing together in the restaurant Fat Fish Blue. However, the bulk of the article told of Maurice's adventures performing on the road, what it was like to play on the street, and similar experiences totally unrelated to either parent. It was the Sax Man's story, not the family's saga.

Then I received the telephone call.

Maurice told me that he had brought a copy of the *Free Times* to show his mother. I had told him the writing approach I had used and had read him a large portion of the final draft, knowing he would otherwise only be able to study the pictures. He had thought it was fair and accurately depicted his career. That was probably why he was laughing so hard as he stood with the telephone in his mother's home, Mrs. Taylor crying so loudly in the background it was uncomfortable to listen. But Maurice was determined I was going to listen, delighted in the dramatic performance I had to experience, a drama that was regularly a part of his adult life.

The outraged, tearful Mrs. Reedus wanted me to know that *she* was responsible for her son's success. *She* had taken him to buy his first saxophone. She had met the payments, and when she needed help, her new husband, *not* Maurice's biological father, was the man who did it. *They* went to the concerts and the band contests (Maurice, Sr., frequently on the road, would still go to see his son perform. He just made certain he was not close to where his ex-wife was sitting.). *They* got him whatever lessons he needed. Without them, Maurice, Jr. would not have succeeded.

There was little to say to Mrs. Taylor as she ranted and cried and tried to make me feel guilty for telling Maurice's story, the one my editor had assigned, and not hers. Later, still experiencing a bit of what in wartime might have been called "shell shock," I talked with long time girlfriends, his ex-wife, and other intimates to the way Maurice and his mother interacted over the years. They felt as I did that she had kept him from reaching his full potential as an individual. They worried about whether or not he could handle truly independent living when she was gone.

As for the Sax Man on that day when he showed his mother the article on his career on the streets, he thought his actions had been a joke on me. Presumably it was.

. . .

"When I was with the Dynamics, I was just like 13 or 14. We all was starting but they [the other musicians] were more advanced than I was [because they could sight read the music]. We all started together in the seventh grade in Rawlings Junior High School Band. We just came out of elementary school and we joined the band. We all started together but I just couldn't comprehend. [My sister] Sharon was with us. She played all through junior high school, from the seventh grade to the ninth grade. 'When I'd be at band rehearsals, they'd always have to remind me which notes to play. I couldn't understand that *they* couldn't understand. I didn't know what was going on, then.

"Everybody in the band, they would always talk about me but they would always keep me around. I guess because I was always funny but they just liked me."

Maurice learned to ask questions about the music. He couldn't read it, and unless he was next to his sister whose fingering he could watch and imitate, he needed someone to show him what to do and explain what was happening. The problem sometimes caused the other kids to tease him or get angry with him, Maurice refusing to tell them the truth for fear it would be proof that he was stupid. At other times the person showing him what to do was patient and unquestioning as to why such help was needed, and the result proved he was a potentially brilliant young musician waiting to happen. Never, though, did Maurice explain he was dyslexic. Worse, neither the teachers nor the doctors his mother took him to see ever explained the condition, that it had nothing to do with intelligence. It would be more than 40 years before Reedus came to understand that he was not stupid, that many men and women achieved greatness while still being dyslexic.

Working with Eddie Smoot and the 5 other conga players was both easier for Maurice than the early days of learning the saxophone and more demanding. The rehearsal time required of each boy was much like he would face as a professional musician, far more intense than what they demanded of themselves when they played in bands of their own creation. Even today, if Maurice is sitting by a table and talking about those early years, his hands start moving in ever more complex rhythms, all part of the Eddie Smoot training five decades earlier. It is a work ethic most observers do not realize he has.

The first gigs for the teenage Maurice, no longer playing exclusively for Eddie Smoot, were much the same as the first professional gigs of older musicians, including his father. You earned your chops playing anywhere, any time - talent shows and birthdays, record hops and school dances, even background music at a party being given by the parents of classmates.

The pay was low to non-existent. Everyone gained critical stage experience, learning to work together playing at the birthday parties of classmates and their siblings. They performed for school canteens (small dances), events where most of the time the boys clustered on one side of the gym and the girls clustered on the other. Everybody looked across the floor, giggling, whispering comments, being too scared to actually ask someone to dance. Hormones might have started raging but they weren't ready to openly touch a member of the opposite sex, a necessity for most of the music of that era. Only later would young teens get in the habit of dancing alone, together. Instead, when they weren't talking about some special boy who didn't yet know girls existed, they would gather around the band, picking their favorites and flirting with the boys, all of whom were classmates, between sets.

The popularity of a band hired to play for canteens for teenagers could lead to more sophisticated work outside of the school setting. There were birthdays and special events, and in the summer this sometimes meant barbecues in the Kinsman and Garden Valley area where he lived. These summer backyard, neighborhood parties allowed the adults to talk, drink beer, and eat whatever had been slow cooked on the grill, while their older children danced to whichever among the latest popular songs the band had mastered.

Maurice and his friends felt they were finding success, though many times the jobs were provided, not because the adults wanted to hear them play but rather to assure the neighbor teens in attendance had something to do other than getting into mischief. But even if the reason for their presence was not always a reflection of their skills, Maurice and his friends were gaining in ability. And if Maurice could not play very well, the others would just play louder, drowning out his mistakes. What mattered to them was that they had become The Dynamics, a part of their first band, a rite of passage for a musician at least the equal of a first meaningful kiss or becoming a licensed driver.

"I remember it being really exciting. I remember trying to impress people and impress my friends. It was like a dream come true. I was actually playing with a band, the first band.

"We used to wear black pants, and what we knew as 'Hi-Boys'—white cotton shirts with big collars on them that we

58

had starched. We went to a clothing store downtown at 9th and Prospect by the Standard Theater where they showed what they called Triple-X rated movies. We used to get all our clothes down there. And across the street from there was Jack Epsteins' [ProspectMusic]." The latter was the store where professional musicians and musicians working to become professionals could buy quality instruments and accessories.

"I was in the Dynamics for the three years I went to Rawlings Junior High. I was still playing with Eddie Smoot and The Courageous Young Men," a fact that became difficult when Rawlings Junior High held a talent show for all the kids who were in bands, singers, dancers, or otherwise had a talent with which they wanted to compete. The Courageous Young Men and The Dynamics were in the show, Maurice effectively competing with himself on two different instruments.

"We [The Courageous Young Men] did talent shows the same day as the Dynamics did one. Smoot, wanting to set apart his boys so they would stand out, "had the idea of two of us in the band being dressed up as Batman and Robin. Since I was real tall, I wanted to be Batman but Eddie wanted us to look awkward so he had me dressed up as Robin, and I was pissed. A real short guy was Batman. We had these outfits on. I'm dressed up like Robin with these tights on. That was so embarrassing, but it was funny to the people.

"We came up [to perform] last, [to perform] and it was weird because I had to go back and put on those clothes, trying not to wear those tights, but I ended up putting them on anyway, and I was the most talked about guy around Rawlings.

"I played with Eddie until almost 17. The musicians who had formed The Dynamics still played in high school, but the boys who had previously used the name The Dynamics had folded and we played in different groups. Mostly we were concentrating and playing in the high school band. And once in a while we would get together and practice a little."

. . .

One of the odd results of the racism that permeated Cleveland and some of the suburbs in those days was the creation of a large number of professional teen musicians. Admittedly there were boys who played one or another musical instruments until discovering an overwhelming desire to pursue the opposite sex at every opportunity. For most of the students who went to Cleveland high schools and had an interest in performing, there were opportunities to perform as an extra-curricular activity, to create their own group and be taken seriously, and even to gain scholarships for music. Parents, teachers, and principals who were frustrated by the regular lack of funds available to students in such suburban high schools as Shaker and Heights were able to provide a professional quality education in music. The result was a disproportionate number of youths who went on to become full time musicians, arrangers, composers, and performers. The Sax Man was a beneficiary of all this.

Playing the after-hours joints

Many of Cleveland's neighborhoods had music, food, and non-alcoholic beverages available in so-called "after-hours joints." Some were the same bars and restaurants where the patrons had been eating and drinking from the time they opened until 2:30 a.m.—closing time for serving alcohol. Others were locations rented for weekends when the late hours did not interfere with jobs and school. And still others were in the large living rooms or recreation rooms of private homes where the owners provided food, soft drinks, and some form of entertainment to whoever came by and paid a small price to get in.

After-hours joints might be considered an adult version of a kid's lemonade stand if the lemonade stand had singers, musicians, and comics in addition to non-alcoholic refreshments. The liquor laws at the time were such that bars could not serve alcohol any later each day than 2:30 a.m. They did not have to close their doors or stop serving their patrons. Soft drinks and package goods or full meals might still be available. In addition, it was legal for private homes to have what amounted to neighborhood after hours joints. The home owner would use a portion of his or her house—living room, recreation room, etc.—and provide food, soft drinks, and some form of entertainment, all available starting at 2:30. In addition there were buildings that could be rented for the weekend.

Some after-hours joints hired professional entertainers for their early morning hours while others took advantage of the fact that regional and national performers who had headlined at major clubs throughout the city often were not ready to return to their hotels. They came to after-hours joints to hold impromptu jam sessions and play-offs much like the competitions that had long been a part of the Great Depression rent parties in New York City's Harlem.

Many of the Cleveland area clubs also offered a third form of entertainment and that was the matinee. Regular entertainment might be available four to five nights a week. After-hours joints opened to the public at 2:30 a.m. but only on those nights when the patrons would not have to awaken in time to go to work or to school. The matinee, by contrast, was usually Saturday or Sunday afternoon.

Sometimes the matinee might truly be an afternoon perfor-mance, the same show available when the club opened in the evening. Other matinees were closer to what was available in the after-hours joints. Musicians would come by and play both with and against one another, competing for audience ap-plause. Comedians would experiment with their jokes, their phrasing, and the attitude they would convey from the stage.

The most cautious of the club owners would limit the teen-age bands to performing no later than 10 P.m. on school nights. Over the years there were efforts to establish curfews for high school students in either the city or the suburbs. This was to assure they did not get in trouble roaming the streets. How-ever, the curfews were usually less restrictive than the teens realized. They required the teen to either be with a responsible adult family member or inside a legitimate business. The teens might get stopped if spotted walking from their homes to the clubs or from the clubs to their homes, but there were no regu-lations that would keep them from performing when they were inside the night spots.

Maurice Reedus never played at night in the after-hours joints, never sneaked out of his home to go to a neighborhood bar to perform the way some of his friends in one or another bands would do. He also did not try to play in the early evenings except when he was living with his father and accompanying the older man to his latest gig. However, he did go to some of the matinees, especially the ones at the Sir Rah House where owner Bob Harris liked to give young performers a chance to hone their craft. And in the case of the young Maurice, Harris gave him the chance to add comedy to his performance abilities.

Chapter Six

East Side/West Side

The teenage Reedus moved among different family members, eventually going to John Adams High School where he became part of the teen band Foreign Blue. The group was a combination of teen musicians from John Adams and boys with whom he had played as part of the Courageous Young Men. What none of them cold realize was how many of them would become regionally, nationally, and/or internationally famous as performers. The 1960s was an era of intense racial unrest and segregation within Cleveland, but it also was an era when every main street had one or more clubs. Some featured jazz. Some had Pop music and Disco. There was Soul. There was Reggae. And many of the clubs had patrons who dressed in sophisticated suits and dresses in the same manner as season regulars attending the world class concerts of the Cleveland Orchestra in Severance Hall.

The major difference among the clubs featuring such entertainment was the same division affecting the rest of the city. The East Side was predominantly Black; the West Side predominantly White. And the Cuyahoga River meandering just off the downtown, a natural break in the region, was the great divide. But since Black acts were barred from white clubs and White acts barred from Black clubs, more talent had to be hired than if the performers could move among all the clubs.

Just meeting the demand for such high end entertainment meant that Cleveland was one of the most desired locations for top name singers, musicians, and comedians. Adding to the acts booked in advance and promoted on WABQ and WJMO, the *Call & Post*, and occasionally one of the Cleveland daily papers were those who showed up for the afternoon jam sessions. Adults, teenagers, and entire families delighted in the range of local musicians proving their skills during the clubs' afternoon off hours.

. . .

Maurice became part of the weekend jam sessions with Foreign Blue, a band whose members included Johnny Britt, a singer with a voice and style that matched that of Michael Jackson. Britt was yet another up- from-the-Cleveland schools entertainer

"He ended up going on a *Temptations* Tour. He was the musical director for the Temptations on one tour. Johnny worked as a trumpet player for one tour with Sly, Slick & Wicked. Now he's doing a lot of studio work." Britt, like other Clevelanders including John Wilson, is multi-talented working as a musician, composer, arranger, and producer. He earned both Gold and Platinum sales when working with the Temptations and

Boney James. He studied in France and helped record artists ranging from Quincy Jones to Jennifer Lopez, the Temptations, and Luther Vandross, among others. And as with Maurice, his earliest training as a musician and performer came as one of the Courageous Young Men.

. . .

In hindsight, the great success young men like Britt, Wilson, and others would have as they became more experienced came, in part, from seeking training to help them hone their talent. Maurice Reedus, Sr. knew his son was inherently talented, knew his son had a gift and a drive to achieve. He also knew that his son's playing was inconsistent, a criticism he would make years later when the band in which Maurice, Sr. played needed another saxophone player and the son wanted to take his place next to his father. The request would be denied, at least one other member of his father's band helping to break the news to the young man. But by then, when Maurice was approaching middle age, there was an arrogance and denial. What Maurice, Sr. had hoped back when his son was graduating from high school was that he would go to college, majoring in music. The older man knew of his son's problems with reading, knew his skill at mastering music he heard, and felt there were professors experienced in helping musicians no matter how they were able to learn. But Maurice would have none of it. His critics said he felt he didn't need the extra schooling. Others recognized that he was afraid of failing and felt destined to do so.

. . .

The first gigs for Maurice were much the same as other, older musicians describe during the time when they were learning to work together. There were canteens—school dances where boys clustered together on one side of the gym and girls clustered together on the other side, looking at each other, giggling, and exploring feelings and emotions that were too new for them to understand. Sometimes a tentative few would dance, usually with each other, and everybody listened to whatever classmates had a band.

The school dances led to being hired for birthday parties or other special events in the lives of the classmates. In summer this sometimes meant barbecues in the Kinsman and Garden Valley area where lived. The backyard parties allowed the adults to talk, drink beer, and eat whatever had been slow cooked on the grill, and the kids danced to whatever of the latest songs the band had mastered.

Maurice and his friends felt they were finding success, not realizing that they were hired because they kept the teens at the parties occupied in ways that were not destructive. But even if the reason for their presence was not a reflection of their skills, Maurice and his friends were gaining in ability. And if Maurice could not play very well, the others would just play louder, drowning out his mistakes.

"I remember The Dynamics being really exciting. I remember trying to impress people and impress my friends. It was like a dream come true. I was actually playing with a band, the first band. We used to wear black pants, white shirts with starched collars. They had shirts called the Hi-Boys—regular cotton shirt with a big collar on it and we had them starched. We went down to the store downtown at 9th and Prospect. Jerry Mills and Belkin's by the Standard Theater. We used to get all our clothes down there. And across the street from there was Jack Epstein's (another popular clothing store for entertainers."

"When I was with the Dynamics, I was just like 13 or 14. We all was starting but they [the other musicians] were more advanced than I was [because they could sight read the music. We all started together in the seventh grade in Rawlings Junior High School Band. We just came out of elementary school and we joined the band. We all started together but I just couldn't comprehend. [My sister] Sharon was with us. She played all through junior high school, from the seventh grade to the ninth grade. 'When I'd be at band rehearsals, they'd always have to remind me which notes to play. I couldn't understand that *they* couldn't understand. I didn't know what was going on, then.

"Everybody in the band, they would always talk about me but they would always keep me around. I guess because I was always funny but they just liked me."

Maurice learned to ask questions about the music. He couldn't read it, and unless he was next to his sister whose fingering he could watch and imitate, he needed someone to show him what to do and explain what was happening. The problem sometimes caused the other kids to tease him or get angry with him. At other times the person showing him what to do was patient and the result was what others saw as a brilliant young musician. Never, though, did Maurice explain he was dyslexic. Worse, neither the teachers nor the doctors his mother took him to see ever explained the condition, that it had nothing to do with intelligence. It would be more than 50 years before Reedus came to understand that he was not stupid, that men achieved greatness while still being dyslexic.

. . .

"I started high school – East Tech and Warrensville Heights High School in 1969 Summer School at John Hay. 1970' They [Sly, Slick & Wicked, the trio of singers who hired Maurice as back-up] had the main guys and needed to put a band together to go on the road.

"We didn't know who Sly, Slick and Wicked was. I had never heard of them. They were just putting a group together to go on the road."

. . .

I was playing the congas. I didn't think I was good enough for the sax. I got the confidence again when I got with Sly, Slick & Wicked. I wasn't playing that much with no band in 1969 and 1970. It took me so long to learn stuff, even the good horn parts, I couldn't believe I learned all those songs for Sly, Slick, and W. I would listen to records. Trying to hear how they were blowing. And then I would always hear something different.

I thought I was playing exactly the way they were. I would play a line and I'd record it and have it on [a little cassette] tape and keep rewinding it back until I'd hear the line over and over again. I had to do a section at a time. It was putting it all together that was the hardest part. It was putting it all together.

"Looking at music for me was like looking at scribble scrabble. If they put the letters on top of the notes I know what they look like. That's what John used to do. He would tell me what to do and I would write them down like an alphabet. I would put down A and then B and the B Flat. I know all the notes. I know how to finger them. Write it out that way and I could follow it. If somebody could write the notes down and then put the note above it. Write down the note and put the note on top of it for the staff.

. . .

"The first out of town job we did was Oberlin College. And we left from there and went down to Lexington, Kentucky. That was back in the early seventies. We did Kentucky a lot. And from Lexington, Kentucky went down to Huntsville, Alabama, Kingsport, Tennessee, Newport, Tennessee, Knoxville, Tennessee, and Mobile, Alabama, and then there was a circuit going back and forth. It was all exciting.

"We ran into the Harlem Globetrotters down in Huntsville. We played this club and they came into the club. We met all the Harlem Globetrotters that were out on the dance floor and backstage with us. The whole team was there.

"We played two clubs in Huntsville. We played one club called The Orbit and then another club was the VFW with Dr. Shabaaz. He was a gay guy who worked at the club. He liked me, though.

"Ladies and gentlemen, the group that brought you 'Surely' and 'Stay My Love,' Paramount recording artists. Can we put our hands together and welcome Sly, Slick, and Wicked." And then we'd start playing and they'd run on stage. Then we'd go into the song. "Surely, you got to make up your mind. Is you is or is you ain't my baby?" The people went crazy about Sly, Slick, and Wicked. I was surprised by how big that record was.

We'd go in and there'd be posters on telephone poles all around the town. It was Sly, Slick & Wicked on the poster. It was exciting. We felt like we was stars. It was big. It was exciting. We was more concerned about the music and remembering our horn lines. But once we really get the show down, we was okay.

"It was exciting. We felt like we was big. Go into a town, we didn't want to leave there. Then you go to the next town and the next town. It was cool. This was the life there. I never wanted it to end. Sleep in a motel room, just kick back and look at TV. Go shopping and stuff like that. Talk to all the girlies."

. . .

"I just got married when I was out of high school. I didn't know Sly, Slick & Wicked when I got married. She wanted me to quit when I got with Sly, Slick & Wicked. She didn't want me to play. We weren't making no big money. She wanted me to work some other job or something. I wanted to travel. I shouldn't have been married. That's all. I got married in 1972 to Birdine."

She got pregnant. She liked me but she tried to kill me. She threw hot water on me. We had just gotten out of high school. She was real insecure. She was real jealous, too. We was always messing around with different women. It was real hard in Cleveland. I was married but I don't think I was in love. I was messing around. Even in high school she wanted to shoot me because I was talking to the home coming queen. Her name was Sharon Taylor, one of the prettiest girls in John Adams. But at the time she had a boyfriend but he wasn't going to that high school. And she had a vehicle. At that time she was the only girl in high school that had a vehicle. We was both seniors. She was the homecoming queen. And then I end up dating one of Sharon's best friends. Her name was Brenda. Brenda kind of hit on me. She liked me. Sharon was pretty from head to toe.

"In the school I was in the John Adams High School Band and then I played with a band on the side, and we all went to John Adams. Saxophone. The Foreign Blue. Everybody went to Adams. The first outside band was the Dynamics in Rawlings Junior High. We did a lot of talent shows. That was kind of hard because I was real slow learning horn parts. Larry, the guitar player, was the leader of the band. He was real smart and knew music real well just like the band teacher. He used to like my sister, Sharon, so he used to work with me and teach me all the horn lines. I used to forget all the horn lines so we'd be on stage doing a show and I was like half blowing my part, pretend I was blowing and I wasn't blowing. It was me... I was playing a baritone sax and a guy named Freddy played tenor sax and Sonny, he played trombone."

. . .

Birdine, the teenager Maurice seduced and who fancied herself in love with him, had gotten pregnant. She did not feel forced to marry the Sax Man. She genuinely loved him and expected him to get a job outside of being a traveling musician, a career neither of them truly understood at that time. According to Reedus, she was insecure and jealous.

"At the time we were always messing around with different women." She was in love with Maurice but he wasn't in love with her. "She wanted to shoot me in high school because I was talking to the home coming queen who liked me—Sharon Taylor. One of the prettiest girls in John Adams High School. She kind of got attached to me. The only girl in high school who had a car. Sharon was pretty, a senior, Home Coming Queen. Then I began dating one of Sharon's best friends, a girl named Brenda."

Maurice was in the John Adams High School Band. Also played in a band on the side – The Foreign Blue. Everyone went to Adams. The first band was in Rawlings Jr. High—The Dynamics—played in talent shows and outside of the school.

"That was hard. I was real slow learning horn parts. But Larry, the guitar player, he was like the leader of the band and he was real smart and knew music really, really well, just like the band teacher. Larry used to work with me and teach me all the horn lines. We'd be on stage doing a show and I'd be like half blowing my part, pretend I was blowing and I wasn't blowing. It was me—I was playing a baritone sax, and a guy named Freddie Kickmore played tenor sax and Jonathon Smith—Sonny—he played trombone. He's big time now. He's in New York an accountant in New York City. He always teases me even when he sees me now—'Maurice, you've come a long way from when you did your one note solos. You're the only guy I knew who did a solo of one note.' I really couldn't play.

There was more to those early days than the problems Maurice had with learning his instrument and mastering any of the music. Junior high is often a time when kids can be insensitive to each other's needs or afraid to be connected with someone who might be the brunt of jokes. The boys knew that Maurice had a famous musician father, a man who traveled the world during his career. They knew that Maurice idolized him, that his taking up the saxophone was mostly because it was the instrument his father played. Yet there seemed no connection between the two Reeduses other than the instrument. Maurice, Jr. played like the kid who is forced to take lessons, dutifully performs at the music teacher's recitals, though hitting flats where sharps belong and sharps where the music calls for flats. A parent might quietly applaud "All them guys could play except for me and they kept me with them. I could never understand that, not even today.

"I was trying to play hard, but my comprehension and forgetting stuff. I was like... They just liked me. Everybody liked me. I was just one of those likeable cats.

"When I was with the Dynamics, we all was starting [as professionals] but they were more advanced than I was. We was maybe like a year into the music, a year into learning how to play. We all started together in the seventh grade in Rawlings Junior High School Band. We just came out of elementary school and we joined the band. We all started together but I just couldn't comprehend. Sharon was with us. She played all through junior high school, from the seventh grade to the ninth grade. [Sharon played the clarinet, an instrument Maurice also learned by watching his sister's fingering. As it happens, the fingering for the clarinet and the saxophone are similar according to musicians who play both instruments.]

"When I'd be at band rehearsals, they'd always have to remind me which notes to play. I couldn't understand that they couldn't understand. I didn't know what was going on, then.

"Everybody in the band, they would always talk about me but they would always keep me around. I guess because I was always funny but they just liked me."

Maurice learned to ask questions about the music. He couldn't read it, and unless he was next to his sister whose fingering he could watch and imitate, he needed someone to show him what to do and explain what was happening. The problem sometimes caused the other kids to tease him or get angry with him. At other times the person showing him what to do was patient and the result was what others saw as a brilliant young musician. Never, though, did Maurice explain he had a problem.

. . .

Reedus moved among different family members, eventually going to John Adams High School where he became part of Foreign Blue. The group was a combination of teen musicians from John Adams and boys with whom he had played as part of the Courageous Young Men. What none of them cold realize was how many of them would become regionally, nationally, and/or internationally famous as performers. The 1960s was an era of intense racial unrest and segregation within Cleveland, but it also was an era when every main street had one or more clubs on what seemed to be every block. There were the weekend nights when the clubs were full of well-dressed men and women, the blacks primarily on the east side and the whites primarily on the west side. Just meeting the demand for such high end entertainment meant that Cleveland was one of the most desired locations for top name singers, musicians, and comedians. Adding to the acts booked in advance and promoted on WABQ and WJMO, the *Call & Post*, and occasionally one of the Cleveland daily papers were those who showed up for the afternoon jam sessions. Adults, teenagers, and entire families delighted in the range of local musicians proving their skills during the clubs' afternoon off hours.

Maurice became part of the weekend jam sessions with

Foreign Blue, a band whose members included Johnny Britt, a singer with a voice and style that matched that of Michael Jackson. Britt was yet another up- from-the-Cleveland schools entertainer.

"He ended up going on a *Temptations* Tour. He was the musical director for the Temptations on one tour. Johnny worked as a trumpet player for one tour with Sly, Slick & Wicked. Now he's doing a lot of studio work."

Britt, like other Clevelanders including John Wilson, is multi-talented working as a musician, composer, arranger, and producer. He earned both Gold and Platinum sales when working with the Temptations and Boney James. He studied in France and helped record artists ranging from Quincy Jones to Jennifer Lopez, the Temptations, and Luther Vandross, among others. And as with Maurice, his earliest training as a musician and per former came as one of the Courageous Young Men.

. . .

"I was playing with Foreign Blue and I was working at Dessel Tool Supply at 38th and Superior. Just a little tool supply, packaging them. They sell nothing but tools. And then I was working in shoe stores. I worked a lot of shoe stores—Kinnie Shoes, Flagg Brothers (Flag) Shoe Store, Thom McCann Shoe Store, Hahn's Shoe Store for Ladies, Higbee's That was like in the late 1960s. I was in school.

"The first real job I had was at a place called Mid-Town Restaurant at 9th Street and Prospect. It was a bunch of Germans who owned it and I was like 14 or 15. Mid-Town Restaurant where Paninni's is now. I washed dishes. 1966,

1968 or later. The food was kind of expensive. Jack Epstein then was on Prospect down at 6th and Prospect.

"Father got first horn from Jack Epstein when he was 16. Epstein's music store. Costello's Music Store around East 105. We had a lot of music stores all around Cleveland in the 1960s. Sam's—sporting equipment (golf) and music.

"We were living with my grandmother Crenell off East 131st one street before Harvard. Fisher's Supermarket at the corner. Before he went on the road. She was crazy man, but I didn't know it. She was real quiet. Didn't smoke no cigarettes. Real soft spoken girl. Real, real quiet. She knows I'm a musician. She just likes me. Had a girl. When she got pregnant she was in the high school. She was a year underneath me. She graduated in 1972. Andrea born in August of 1972. We just went to a justice of the peace. Me, my grandmother, and my father. Didn't want to go downtown. I think my mother was at work for General Electric.

Chapter Seven

Two Dreams:
One for Himself and One for his Father

"I always wanted to be like my father. My father was a saxophone player and he played the saxophone from the time I was born. I was crazy about my father and he was a full time musician. I liked the way he walked. I wanted to walk like him. I wanted to talk like him. I wanted to talk like him, and I wanted to wear the same clothes he wore. He was just so cool. I thought that man was the coolest man in the world. I think that way today. "He used to play at the clubs around Cleveland. He played Gleason's.

He played the Twist Bar on the west side. He did some stuff for (singer/ television variety show host Mike Douglas. I remember when I was a kid he was on the Mike Douglas Show playing saxophone a couple of times. He was always going on the road traveling. He did the jazz concerts that Channel 5 had in the late 1950s and early 1960s."

The elder Reedus was traveling around the United States with a group called the Lonny Woods Trio at the time. He was one of the area's most versatile saxophone players including having been the only musician in his high school who had been able to play Be-Bop, a style promoted by Charlie Parker. He had been in his school's marching band, and his son had heard that all the other musicians in his father's high school had wanted to play just like him.

The elder Reedus had also done whatever was necessary to hear live music when he was still in school. Maurice, Jr. said, "He used to go to the Masonic Temple at 36th and Euclid and sneak in the back door because Charlie Parker was playing there. He'd talk with Charlie Parker, Miles Davis. Daddy was strictly a jazz musician. (He) talked real jazzy. Straight A student in school."

. . .

"I played with Eddie until almost 17. The musicians who had formed The Dynamics still played in high school, but the boys who had previously used the name The Dynamics had folded and we played in different groups. Mostly we were concentrating and playing in the high school band. And once in a while we would get together and practice a little." There were also side trips for Maurice to wherever his father was living or working. And when the younger man became too anxious, he would not wait for his father to pick him up. He would start walking in what he hoped was the right direction such as when he surprised his father in Omaha.

. . .

Maurice Reedus, Sr. — I was driving along and there was Maurice [Junior] on the corner of Longwood and Denny Streets in Omaha, Nebraska. I said, 'Where in the world?' He come down and stay with me a while. He was down in Columbus a couple of times. And then in California, I went out there to play at the clubs around LA and San Francisco, Sausalito, about three years. First time I saw Redd Foxx personally in Los Angeles and then in Cleveland. Dionne Warwick and Redd Foxx over on Wilson Mills now closed down. This was 1970, 1971 or 1972. The Temptations came there. Off of 271. Stage that circled around. 1972-1975. I've been in every state in the United States except North Dakota. It was a hell of a trip when I went to Missoula, Montana. Played the colleges.

"Texas was bad, too. We had shootings when we played there. [Trying to get a job with a band just before the Korean War started.] Somebody come in shooting. Ducking under chairs. I was gone. I told the cat, service makes me nervous. This was 1950. August 29 I was in the service jumping out of airplanes

"I did most of my traveling between the age of 25 and 45. It was like downhill all the way. Came back to Cleveland and started working for Mutual Benefit Life on 9th in the Hanna Bldg. Selling insurance. Got a broker's license. Sold for Equity insurance. Doing it on my own. I was working on the company but I got more time to play. Selling policies like for 10,000 or better. I had to meet most of my clients in the bars. I was drinking. That was sort of messing around with me with gigs. Equitable Insurance and Mutual Benefit Life." Fortunately he got himself dried out and let his showmanship delight most audiences. As he explained:

"We did skits.

Sometimes he would wear clothing that made him look like a rube and he would be in the back of the audience. He'd wander back and forth, finally saying, "Boo! Boo!"

Then, when the straight man on stage, seemingly unfamiliar with the man mocking him, would stop playing his instrument, Maurice would ask, "What's going on in back of that bandstand?" The seemingly annoyed straight man would say, "Ain't nothing going on."

And Maurice would follow with "Ain't nothing going on in front of it, either." Then the seemingly annoyed straight man would tell Maurice that if he thought he could do better, he should come up on stage. And that's where the comedy would begin.

"1960s started the comedy. Short stand-up with Hamp. Instead, if something happened on the grandstand. A drummer would have a skin break or something. I would just fill in until he got straight. I just got up and did it. I'd go and say, "Ladies and Gentlemen, we had a little mishap here so I'll entertain you as best as I can. It's nice looking down into some of your faces. Some of your faces could really stand some looking down into. There are some ugly people in here this evening. If you don't believe me, just look next to you. Go ahead, take a chance.

"It's nice being here this evening. In fact, I'm glad to be anywhere this evening. My landlord told me that if I wasn't here this evening, I'd disappear from there tomorrow evening.

I wasn't doing it alone by myself. The band was always there so I just made it a part of the act. We'd play. Then we'd do that act. Then I'd do the stand-up. Then we had a female vocalist and she'd do her thing. And then we'd just go back around again. We did jazz. We did the blues. We did the R&B. We had everyone on the band

I'd say, 'I wish I was a dog and you were a tree." Or "I'll come down there to your mouth and cut your sex life off." "You'd get mad if I came down to your job and took away your mop and broom." I didn't have that many hecklers. At the start of the comedy, John would be there on the stage with a hat on. I'd be coming from the back. I'd have these great big long overalls on and a big old hat, and a cigar inside my face, acting like I was drunk."

"He'd say, 'Oh, man, you're drunk."

"I'd say, "You're ugly."

"Yeah, but you're drunk." "But you're ugly."

"You're drunk."

"Yeah, but in the morning I'll be sober."

"I'd put on a Batman suit. I'd take it off and under that thing I'd have my suit on. Summer time I'd be coming in the front door, staggering."

"I'll have the bouncer throw you the hell out of here."

"No bouncer threw me the hell in here. He won't throw me the hell out of here."

"We had a lot of fun. Keep it lively. Don't let anyone get bored.

"The stand-up thing I'd do that as part of the band thing. I'd take 15 or 20 minutes and get them going that way."

. . .

The early days:

"Me and the organ player used to play at a place called Memories on Brecksville. You come off of 480 or right around the corner from the vets' hospital. We occasionally play there as a dual. Most of the people like us but there's still some idiot somewhere. Like we were playing there two or three weeks ago and two cats back there were sitting, talking to each other. I know they've been there before because we'd seen them there before, so I think they were maybe friends of the bartender or friends of one or two of the bar girls who work there.

"All of a sudden the joint got quiet for a minute and one of them said, 'Nigger!' real loud, and everybody heard it. Nobody else say anything. And one of the girls said, "No! No! Take it outside. They were probably talking to each other about something else, but at the time it came out, things just happened to be quiet, and I thought...'Oh, boy...' And that's what it's like today, but a whole lot better. You know, a newer generation. "I was saying some jokes before and they wouldn't like I was doing them. We was talking about color in some kind of way. I would say, like,

"My parents were mixed. I don't know which side to hate."

"It's hard when your parents are mixed because you wake up in the morning with the taste in your mouth of filet mignon and biscuits. Pheasant and black eyed peas.

"I don't care what color you are. When it comes to going to bed and turning out the light, it becomes a question of who washed.

"You get it in through your comedy because it takes the truth to tell a joke. "What's the difference between a joke and a wise crack? A joke is a woman who has ten kids and a wise crack is a woman who has none."
You have to think. It might be too much for you.

"I wasn't in there when you had to get off the bus and not go into the restroom.

"When I first started playing 77th and Detroit. I had to play four years at $10 a week."

. . .

"1975 went down to the valley and ended playing with Jimmy Smith the organ player. Met Robert Lockwood, Jr. in 1972. When he came back to Cleveland in 1980 he made that the focus. Just started traveling with Robert. We didn't play in Cleveland other than little joints like Peabody's, the Cove down in the Flats. All the factories were down there then.

"Then we played the Flip Side on Mayfield. We'd go to New York, and Rochester, and Buffalo. And then we did the outside concerts. Went to Ann Arbor and every year we'd go to the Chicago Blues Fest, the Montreal Blues Fest. All the festivals so we still were based right here.

When I came back to Cleveland in 1971 for a minute. The drummer, George Cook was blind. He came to Cleveland. Playing with Robert. That was in 1971.

"I went over to his house one day. 'I hear you play saxophone.' 'I hear you play guitar.' He told me about his Delta roots. He also played jazz. Started mixing jazz and the blues.

Played all four parts on the guitar. Different from BB King. Could never play clubs because the younger generation didn't want to hear it. Black clubs would have tossed them out. Robert never got national attention. Went to white clubs. Eric Clapton began imitating. He kept working but I don't know.

"Quit playing for ten years. Drove school bus. Drove delivery for a drugstore. Shooting pool.

"The first time I played Severance Hall. People dug it. We

played four times. Each time it was full."

. . .

During this same period, Maurice, Jr. often moved back and forth between Cleveland and wherever his father was living, the older man giving his son additional experience in the local clubs. "It was 1967. I was 14 years old and going to stay with my father in Columbus for the first time. He was playing at a club called the Cadillac Club as part of a group called the New Fools, and it was at that club that he met another band. They played a gig there. They're like 19, 20, 21... They're out of school. They were called the Instrumentals and I got to rehearse with that band every day. It was a big band. They had like a four piece horn section. Lead guitarist, keyboard...big band. I'm like a kid and they let me practice with them. I sat in with them during an afternoon jam session and they were really impressed by the way I played the Congas. I took my drums up there with my father and I sat in with them and I played with them.

"They kind of took me underneath their arm and I started rehearsing with them.

"There was a jam session during the day and in the evening they had their gig. I sat in with their jam sessions. I could sit in. Play with them. They were a Top 40 band. I had two congas and I set up next to the drummer. It was like Tower Power and Earth, Wind, and Fire.

"I really wanted to play the horn but I only had it for one year and when I went to Columbus, the school I went to in Columbus didn't have no band. But I still played the Congas. "My father let me go out and I did a couple of shows with them, a lot of festivals downtown. My father let me do stuff that I couldn't do with my mother, Anita Hightower Reedus Taylor.

"That was the very first band I played with. I was like, hey man! This is a real band. They paid me cash. They got paid $50 each, I might have got paid $15 or $20. That was a lot of money to me. I never played with a real band before, too. They would come pick me up. Daddy had left me to go on the road and I was staying with my stepmother. They'd pick me up after school. Sometimes we'd rehearse in the Poindexter Recreation Center in Columbus."

. . .

"1967 in Columbus Ohio. My father was playing the Cadillac Club when he was with the group The New Fools. It was a band that I met and played a gig there. These guys were 19, 20, 21 but I got a chance to rehearse with this band every day. The Instrumentals. I went to the matinee. They had a four piece horn section, lead guitar, key board. Like Tower Power, a big band. I was like a kid and they let me practice with them. I sat in with them at a jam session. I took my drums with me and sat in with them. I started rehearsing with them—the afternoon matinee. Jam session during the day and gig in the evening. Sat in and played with them. They played Top 40 band. Tower Power—look up. I played the Congos. I had two Congos and I set up next to the drummer. I wanted to learn how to play the horn but I had only played one year. My father used to allow me to go out and do a couple of shows with them, festivals. And for me being 14 my father let me do stuff that I couldn't do when I was living with my mother.

"That was the very first band I ever played with—The Instrumentals. They paid me cash. Back in them days, in the sixties, it might have been they got paid $50 and I got $15 of $20.

"When Daddy went on the road, I was staying with my stepmother and they would come pick me up. Sometimes we would rehearse at the Poindexter Recreation Center in Columbus. I went to junior high school in Columbus for about six months. I had left playing with Eddie Smoot and all and I was playing with a real band.

"It kept me occupied because I thought I was going to be with my Daddy, but he was only there two or three months before he went on the road. I got to do stuff I could never did if I was with my mother. I played with the band, smoked cigarettes and all. I couldn't do that. I had my own bedroom and a record player and my little transistor radio, 8 track tapes. I could play all night.

"I remember always getting standing ovations [when playing the congas with The Instrumentals]. They always gave me a lot of solos. It was just I wanted to be big. They were older [interested in girls] and I was just a kid.

"I didn't talk with no girls anyway. I wasn't doing none of that. I didn't know what to say to them anyway. What was I going to say? I gotta go home? I got to go to school. I'm a kid. Anybody could look at my face and tell I was young. I had a smooth face.

"I tried to act like I was older. I used to drink something, act like drinking but don't be drinking. I'd be drinking a drink like I'm drinking a drink and don't be drinking nothing. I don't drink. I never drink. I used to fake it all the time."

. . .

"They used to have a Jazz Matinee around three or four o'clock on Sunday afternoons. It could be jam packed in there, too. They had liquor. It was a bar. It's called Jazz Matinee. My father played there in the afternoon and then had to come back at night to play. The matinee was for all the musicians to play and jam. It was like 4 to 7, and then they'd come back and play again like from around 10 o'clock until 2:30. The musicians would get paid for the evening but they didn't get paid for the matinee. They'd just come in and jam. I would go up and play with my father. I never rehearsed with him. I'd just go up there and he let me play. I think I got with Eddie Smoot when I was 12 or 13.

"I had to leave the group, The Courageous Young Men, when I went to Columbus for about six months. I went right back. I was always the tallest one, the tallest kid in the group. "And Eddie Smoot, he'd always be on me all the time. I just tried to play my drums exactly like he played his [drums]. I think I was the only one in the group who played just like Eddie Smoot. I wanted to play exactly like him because he could play. I copied him. I put my hands on the drums the same way he would put his hands on the drum.

"Eddie would send us home. We would practice on a table, on the chairs, Practice cupping our hand, doing rolls with our fingers.

"Back then I didn't care about the audience. It was just being on stage with my father that was cool.

"Only thing it was I just knew I was going to be playing with my Dad. I used to go there (the clubs) and just listen to him. I wasn't playing the horn then. I was just hearing the drums. I just knew if I could hear the song I knew what kind of beat to play. Daddy would give me solos all the time. I felt so confident about my solos I couldn't wait for the people to hear them. They were crazy about my father so I used to get a lot of attention from all his friends. They gave me a lot of attention. I used to try and wear his clothes. I remember one time he gave me one of his suits. Man, I made that suit fit me. It didn't fit me but I just made it fit me. I couldn't wait to wear it, wear it to school to show everybody 'cause I could see him wear that suit on stage. When he was living in Manhattan, New York, he sent me the pictures with that suit on. It was a gold, pinstripe suit. All three of them had the same color suit. It was a silk suit. It was silk, gold, with the black pin stripe.

"My father had a record out. It came out in maybe '67' or '66.' It was Spotlight Record of the Week on WABQ (Cleveland radio station). It was an instrumental called Sassafras featuring Maurice Reedus, so he did have a solo record. It was *Sassafras* on the first side of the record, and then you turned it over and there was more *Sassafras—Sassafras Part 2*.

. . .

Kelvin Taylor

Kelvin Taylor, the one legged man was different. He rarely played with others because he was still trying to master the fundamentals of the music he loved. Practice sessions were often in the RTA bus stop shelter, not on a stage or in a recording studio. The sounds he produced were sometimes masterful, more often pedestrian, and occasionally painful to hear. He had no illusions about his skill, however. He worked steadily at his craft, hearing increments of improvement day after day, the reward for the effort expended.

For the one-legged man a life focused on mastering his music, then sharing each new achievement with strangers on the streets, provided the emotional satisfaction needed to get through each day. The only bands he joined were ones put together with other men in similar circumstances, one struggling with a trumpet, another with a guitar or other instrument. The ad hoc groups were sometimes seen outside the Cleveland Browns Stadium, well away from the Sax Man who also appeared at such venues. There was no rivalry with the Sax Man. They knew he had played in locations they could only fantasize about. They did not play where passers-by would have to choose between them. They sought only to share their love, not compete. They lived to play their music on the streets.

By contrast the Sax Man wanted to return to the days of limousine transports, hotel room "homes," and a constantly changing string of cities, nightclubs, stadiums and women... The Sax Man wanted more than anything else to return to the road trips like a   star.

. . .

"We changed clothes three times a night. We did three shows. We had three different sets of uniforms. Each time we'd go down to the dressing room to change clothes we'd do our little thing or whatever and then everybody had their ladies out front. And we'd go out and say 'Hi.' Didn't nobody know this. Only certain people down there in the dressing room with us. There wouldn't be any women. Only all men. Anybody had their girlfriends with them, they'd be out sitting at the table in the audience. We had different shows with different songs.

We'd have a rehearsal and we'd add new songs to a set.

"We had certain songs. Like show 1, we're going to do like eight songs. Show 2 would be a different type of song. Show 3 was different. We had about 8 songs in a set. Every show we did three sets. All the songs we did was good songs. All three songs was hot. [There was never an attempt to relax because the later night crowd might be drunk.]

The second set would be more smoking, like maybe more dance songs. "Sir Rah House didn't have a dance floor. They had tables. The band would sit up on a small stage area. We was like a show band. People would sit down and listen to the show. Didn't nobody dance. When we played Players Lounge, they had a big dance floor. Players Lounge. That was a real big club down in Akron. We did a lot of Earth, Wind and Fire type songs. We was like the Ohio Players—a big horn band. There wasn't a song we couldn't do because we had so many horns."

. . .

The 1975 Kool Jazz Festival would prove to be the treasured beginning of the Sax Man's years of triumph during which he played behind or alongside some of the most celebrated greats in rhythm and blues, rock, and jazz. He traveled the country with one group or another, going from club to club, hotel room to hotel room. The good times brought income others would look upon with envy. The bad times came with cheating club owners, corrupt managers, at least one shared meal of a single slice each of a carefully divided piece of Fleer's Double Bubble Chewing Gum while the musicians waited for their expense money to arrive a few hours later.

And always there were the unexpected problems with fans, such as a gun toting irate husband blaming one of the traveling musicians for the misbehavior of his adulterous wife.

The road was tiring yet always an alluring adventure. Money might be short at times, usually because a crooked manager pocketed too large a portion of the box office receipts or house guarantee, but there was always food, cleaned and pressed clothing, and a bed on which to lay your head. It was a life seemingly without responsibilities other than to learn the music, show up, and perform. And because most of the musicians were barely past puberty, their still raging hormones found an outlet with the local girls who were projecting their own fantasies on to the Sax Man and his fellow performers.

The Sax Man's experiences as a traveling musician seemed unique to his life and times. It was as though he was a living Ken Doll for young women transitioning from playing with Barbies to plastering their bedroom walls with posters of their favorite celebrities to actually bedding a musician after he performed at their favorite club. Maurice, like other young performers, was delighted to let himself be seduced as often as possible in the towns where they played.

It helped the Sax Man's technique that he was tall, reed thin, and playing what is arguably one of the most seductive sounding instruments in any band. The result was that he was the frequent focus of a barely legal female patron's attention, and a not much older jealous male's wrath. Despite the tension he might create, the Sax Man would often go sit with one or another of the female members of the audience when he was between numbers. And if circumstances were right, he would share his hotel room until it was time to get ready to go to the next club in the next town.

The women knew nothing of the lives of the band members when they weren't in the club performing. Often they only knew a musician's first name or the nickname used when he was introduced to the audience during a set. Their actions were foolish, but the clubs held the ambiance of raging hormones, the most powerful counter to common sense experienced by teenagers and young adults everywhere.

The musicians were equally unknowing about the girls they met. They often acted impulsively, and as a result, most of the time the term "safe sex" came to mean keeping an eye out for a boyfriend, a husband, or in some cases, a parent. They carried condoms and tried to find a way to have access to penicillin when on the road, the medication a back-up in case "getting lucky" actually meant not getting quite so lucky after all. And to assure peak performance as both singers and lovers, there were street drugs made available to them in their dressing rooms.

. . .

I was in a ten piece band called the Metronomes. When we played at a club called the Native Son, the dressing room was down in the basement. Out of the ten of us, maybe nine of us was doing cocaine. Sometimes we'd bring our own. Sometimes the man—Willy Cooper—would bring it. He was our supplier. He went south to live. Haven't seen or heard of him in years. He liked our music and he would be at the club to see the show. But before shows started or between shows he'd come downstairs to the dressing room and all the band members would line up like a football team. He would give us drugs at the start of the show and we would pay him at the end of the night when we got paid. He had cocaine lines for us to snort and we were smoking it, too. Sometimes we'd be carrying our clothes [to get dressed for the show] and we'd be passing it around.

I remember this one particular time everybody was lined up so we could go out one at a time until everybody was on stage. It was some song where the instruments were on the stage and one person would go out and start. Then the next person would go out and join him. Then the third person until we were all playing on the stage.

As we started out we'd pass where lines of coke were laid out with a soda straw nearby. There were 10 lines laid out and a straw that was passed from one person to the next. You'd snort your line, grab your horn, and start to play on stage. The lines were precut and big. Ten lines—big old lines, too. He pre-cut it and set it out. He didn't tell us how much it was going to be. Sometimes he'd just give it to us on the house.

The first show... it was free. But the second show when we'd do it again, he'd be down there all night long, getting it to them as they came off and went on stage until we got through playing. Then they had to pay up.

We'd always talk about getting it on credit. He always came to the show. Some of the members of the band would get extra coke on credit. He'd always come to the gig. Some of the members would pay first. Some would pay last. Some people owed anyway. Some people got a little extra and they might owe from the last gig. He never raised the price.

Back then we'd be buying like $25 worth, $30 worth or whatever. And he knew we was just playing music [no other source of income] so he wouldn't press us about our money. He would never press us. But when we came into town, he was always at the show. He was always at the show with it (cocaine). At the off time we would go to his house.

Sax Man blowing changes

The drugs, the women, the travel... They were all distractions for a musician barely out of high school. Most of those young band members avoided physical and emotional commitments when they first started playing and touring professionally. A few became serious about a young woman who was more than a fan, more than a distraction, but someone who understood the stresses and temptations and accepted the risk. There was even the occasional married entertainer who would telephone his wife or lover when he landed a relatively lengthy gig in a town filled with distractions. Get on the next plane (or bus, as the case might be) and come down here. There are a lot of beautiful women. There are a lot of willing women. I'm lonely and I don't want to lose what we have.

The entertainers who sent for their wives were the exception, and the singers and musicians who requested their presence usually were older and had either seen or experienced a marital break-up they did not want to repeat.

The Sax Man's solution he thought was perfect. The clubs are dangerous, he told Birdine, the young woman he married just out of high school when hormonal lust overwhelmed either of their common sense. They're in bad parts of the city and the people who go there are often drinking too much. He couldn't protect her while he was performing so it was best if she just stayed home so he wouldn't worry.

Maurice's wife was no fool. She had gone to those same clubs as soon as she was of legal age. She had been in those same neighborhoods without incident. The only reason her husband might not want her presence was because he was hiding something. That was when she went to the club where the Sax Man had his next gig, sitting well to the back where he would not see her.

To the Sax Man's regret, he sat next to a woman in the audience and began touching and kissing her. His wife watched just long enough to be certain he was the aggressor, then charged at him, chasing him through the kitchen. She chased him around the kitchen and then back out the door.

Chapter Eight

Yes, I'm Married, but...

Girls and the night and the Sax Man

"I was with the Metronomes, a nine piece band and we were doing R&B and Pop. We was in the Sir Rah House.

"We did a lot of cameo stuff. Tower of Power stuff. I was on the stage and there was three women who came to the club. I had been dating all three and they all came to see me. I was scared to come out there."

The women were sitting around the club in a way that prevented Maurice from getting past them. *"I had to leave out the back door of the club. I was lucky because it was like the third set going into the last set of the night. I had three of the guys go to two of the tables to talk with them."*

Maurice was at the third table with a woman named Rochelle who was sitting at an angle that her back was to what was happening at the other tables. However, he knew that she personally knew the *other girls and if she turned around, she would see them. I told her I was going to the bathroom and she was sitting so her back was facing us. If she had turned around...*

"*I had three women in the same club and didn't know they were coming, and one of them was a police girl for the Fourth District. She had her uniform on and everything.* "*It was big, man, and I was scared to death. The place was packed. I'm sitting on stage trying to play. I had a glass that saved me.*

"*You know how the girls be screaming. We're the type of group like we had a guy singing like Eddie Kendricks. We had steps. Nice uniforms, red and leather stuff... Spandex tights with the chain belt and all.*

"*I was like really frightened because I didn't know what to do. I left out the back door. I knew where they were sitting at and each one of them know me.*

"*Back then they knew me, they knew how I used to act on stage. I didn't even change clothes. I went backstage, I put my horn in the case, and left all my clothes. I told Pete I had to go meet my father and he wasn't even in town. I was staying with my grandmother at the time.*

"*I went to my grandmother's house and told my grandmother and she laughed.* "*I told my grandmother everything because one time they both came over to her house. I looked out the window and they were both parked out there. They were both standing on my grandmother's porch but I wasn't there. I was up in the attic.* "*At the club they asked, 'Where is Maurice?' and they were told, 'He left with his father.'*

"*But in the morning two of them came over to my grandmother's house. Linda and Rochelle. At my grandmother's house and they knew I was in my grandmother's house but she wasn't even there. They just went up on the porch and told me, 'You've got to make a* choice. It's either me or it's her' and they're both looking at me.

"I thought they were going to kill me, brother. That was my thinking. I was very, very nervous. So I guess they had both been talking.

"I really didn't say nothing. I didn't make no choice. Back then I was like more scared. I was the guy who was always shy. I didn't know how to talk with women. "I see some guys talking with women and I'll be like, 'how can he talk to her like that?' And they'd tell them anything and the women would believe it. I just couldn't do anything like that. That's when this lying came out of me. I start making up excuses—Well, I'm over here and I'm over there. And like he's seeing four or five women and he's over at her house and they've got kids. A lot of guys did that but I wasn't like that. I was trying to be big but I wasn't.

"I was in the house and I was asleep. My wife boiled a whole pot of water and she poured the water on my face. I had first degree burns on the whole side. I got one of those flop hats you used to wear back in the seventies so I could go on tour with the O'Jays then. Then I had a bandage over this side of the face."

[Years later the woman who cared for him the longest commented: When I met him he was going with Rochelle. That was a sex party. We are not committed. We're just dating. We hadn't decided if we were going to be committed. Then I realized I was going to be in it for the long haul so I said to him, "Do you want me to speak to her? And just suddenly out of the blue he said (on the phone to Rochelle) don't call me on the phone no more. I've finally got somebody that love me. And we're just getting ready to go to one of his gigs. She didn't call him no more. And he told me last year, Babe, he said, her and her husband came to the place and she looked at me like I wasn't and I looked at her like she wasn't. But he said he's supposed to have a child by her and she told him that she never wanted *this child. It was his, but yet she called him to come to his school to see the child in a play.*

. . .

"I was living in the projects down here on Cedar and 22nd. And [my wife] took my saxophone and tore it up, brother. Banged it. The railing in the projects—they got those steel railings in the projects for when you go up the steps. Smashed it up, brother. I took it to the shop and the guy said there wasn't nothing he could do with it (the sax) except use it for other pieces. It was that messed up. He said there was nothing he could do with it. I had first degree burns all over my right side."

. . .

Another time during those early years of going from group to group and playing in the smaller clubs Maurice was flirting with girls between sets. They were young, noisy, and hoping to go home with one of the band members. That was when his wife arrived. She was extremely angry but it was not obvious what her intentions might be until she walked over to him and pulled a gun out of her purse.

"I really didn't know that she was so jealous. She would just come in and let everybody know 'that's my mister.' She'd just talk out loud. If she saw a girl looking at me, she'd say, 'Why is she looking at you like that?'

"I don't know. I'm up on the stage."

. . .

"I was playing the Checkmate Lounge at Shaker Square around 1970. I was up there doing my comedy routine. I was talking about my wife. It was funny. When she walked in I was just saying, 'You all got to see my wife to believe in Halloween.' I didn't know that she was coming in to shoot me on the stage. She had been following me but I didn't know she was following me. When I got out of a club, she'd be parked where she could see every move I made. She never found anything out, but then I found out one of the guys in the band was letting her know the information [about the women I was seeing]. Back then I wasn't doing too much in Cleveland. I was the only one in the band who was married.

"I was married at 19. I married her because she was pregnant. I got her pregnant. She was still in high school. I just didn't get a chance to do a lot of things because when they used to go out (after playing), I was married.

"Back when we was young, I was like a wild person with women.

"The boiling water attack was similar to what had taken place on October 18, 1974, when singer Al Green, back from a San Francisco concert, was taking a bath in his Memphis, Tennessee home when Mary Woodson forced her way inside. She was a New Jersey woman, married with children, and a lover of his music. She had seen him perform in upstate New York, eventually following him to Tennessee where he lived.

"The New Jersey woman was a fan who was married with children. She left her family and attended a Green concert in upstate New York), and traveled to Tennessee, entering his home and taking a boiling hot container of grits, poured it on his body. Then she fled into one of his bedrooms, took his gun, and killed herself." The assault against Green was believed by the singer to have been punishment from God for straying from his commitment to religious music. Oth-

101

ers felt he had simply been stalked by a violent fan with whom he had had an affair, one of any number of women with whom he had been involved in the past. Whatever the case for Green, the woman who attacked him knew that the unmarried Green had been seeing others. Maurice's wife only knew of his affairs second hand, at least according to his friends.

Whether Maurice's wife got the idea for the boiling liquid attack from the actions of Al Green's murderous fan is not known. Maurice was upset about his wife because, as he later explained, "she did it on hearsay. She had heard he was doing this or doing that. What she was getting information from was somebody in the band."

But was the information accurate? Was he cheating on her? "At that particular time she was right because I was trying to be like everybody else in the band, and at that particular time and ain't nobody else married in the band but me. But she couldn't know, though.

"I had everybody in the band helping me out and one person pushing her buttons. It was one of the singers, too. You knew how singers are. The girls was always out after the singers.

The contentious marriage lasted four years from ceremony to divorce though they were separated the last year. Maurice could not wait to date others, though, and since he was living in his father's house while the terms of divorce were worked out, he saw no reason not to take up with someone new. This time his choice was a woman who owned a brand new Mustang she parked in front of his father's house.

Maurice's soon-to-be-ex-wife pulled up in front of his father's house when she spotted the Mustang. She stopped her car, then floored the accelerator, smashing into the Mustang. Next she put her car in reverse, again flooring the engine. Back and forth. Back and forth. Fenders crumpled, glass broke, the doors caved in, fluids leaked onto the street. The car was not going to be driven anywhere again without a major overhaul.

The problem as Maurice's ex-wife saw it was that her husband could not be trusted. Matters were made worse when he was playing locally and told her the club where he was performing was a rough one. It was too dangerous for her to go there, certainly too dangerous for her to be inside watching him play.

The Sax Man's wife would hear none of what she knew was nonsense. If there was a problem with the club, it was that there were sections of the audience in shadows such that the patrons could see and hear everything going on stage but the performers were blinded by the harsh lights. His wife watched him leave the stage after the band's set and any comedy he performed, then move to a table where another woman was waiting to hold him, kiss him, and promise an intimacy yet to come. Worse, it was obvious that this was not a first night pick-up.

Livid, Maurice's enraged wife began chasing him in the club. He escaped into the kitchen where the manager was desperate to have them stop the battle. He wanted no one hurt in his club. He wanted no bad publicity. But when his wife picked up a massive cooking pot filled with hot liquid, all the manager and kitchen staff could do was watch helplessly as she tossed it on the Sax Man.

Later the men from the band as well as other musicians and friends of the couple talked about what they had seen. One quiet, laid back horn player asked what, for him, seemed the obvious question. "Did he kill the bitch?"

. . .

The Sax Man never complained about what happened, admitting years later that he deserved the harsh reaction, and his ex-wife confirmed her actions when questioned about them.

She also mentioned the night she tried to hit him with her car when he went out to the parking lot, and another time when the bodyguard for the singing group the O'Jays did a routine check of all purses and handbags brought backstage by family and fans. Maurice's wife was carrying a handgun that the bodyguard quietly confiscated.

Fortunately for both Maurice and his wife, a divorce seemed more sensible than a long term jail sentence. But through to this day, each time a woman fancies herself in love with the Sax Man, Maurice is as faithful as the time they are physically together. Or as the song about less than constant lovers that Frank Sinatra made famous states, "when he's not with the one he loves, he loves the one he's with."

Chapter Nine

Kansas City

In many ways Maurice's actions were understandable though obviously not laudable. His marriage lasted from 1972 to 1976 though he was actively dating others the last year as the terms of the divorce were worked out. This was also a time when he was traveling the country, sharing the stage with such famous groups as the Ohio Players, Count Basie, and numerous others. Referring to his short term wife, he noted that he was 19 years old, in hindsight little more than a kid. "When I first married her I was with Sly, Slick & Wicked and the O'Jays. I got a chance to walk Ella Fitzgerald to the stage. It was an honor. It was the Playboy Jazz Fest in a suburb of Los Angeles. I was backstage with John Wilson and I was dating Duke Ellington's daughter from his second marriage—Elisha Ellington. Jimmy Witherspoon. He was their godfather. He was a real big blues singer. Spoon...

"The biggest compliment I ever got was from Count Basie. It was a tune by Major Harris called 'Love Won't Let Me Wait.' Harris was in the group The Delphonics. In that song is a saxophone solo."

The year was 1975. Maurice was playing his saxophone as a back-up for Sly, Slick & Wicked. The trio and their musicians were in Kansas City, Missouri, at the newly opened Kansas City Royals Stadium which was packed with more than 80,000 people attending the Kool Jazz Festival.

The musicians shared a dressing area with sheets dividing the groups for what passed as privacy. When it was their turn to play, golf carts took them from the dressing area, across the field, and to the stage.

The technology that now seems dated was new then. There were several cameras spotted around, all with zoom lenses to capture changing action and different points of view. There was a massive screen on which whatever a camera captured at the director's guidance was suddenly many times bigger than life on that screen.

The Sax Man hadn't noticed the screen at first. What he saw was a cheering crowd excitedly waiting to be entertained by the musicians. Then he glanced up at the screen.

"They had just built the stadium. I'm looking at myself on this big screen like a movie screen.

"I can't mess up this solo. All these people..."

Reedus didn't mess up the solo. Terrified, he gradually relaxed as the music flowed from his sax as perfectly as he had practiced, as brilliantly as any musician present that day. The only time he almost lost emotional control was when he glanced back at the giant screen. The director had cued one of the camera operators to focus on Maurice's hands as he fingered the keys of his saxophone. The image was as visually dramatic as the notes he was playing, and when he finished, the 80,000 jazz fans in attendance rose as one.

Reedus, grinning, thrilled to have the rest of the group by his side, watched a wave of people standing, applauding, whistling, cheering, roaring their respect for a teenager whose dyslexia left him incapable of reading the glowing reviews in the next morning's newspaper and a group of young musicians conquering the world on their first tour.

When Maurice was returned to the dressing area and the next band took the stage, Count Basie walked over to him and said, "That was a lovely solo. You did a good job."

"I couldn't believe it. We're talking about the Count. You know who played with Count Basie? All of the greats and he's shaking my hand.

"I'm like 19 years old. And I'm already feeling guilty about things. I didn't consider myself a top notch saxophone player at all. I'm still learning. My reading on the part... I'm playing by ear and everybody's telling me how it sounds. And to me, it's I can't play the way they play. Every horn player can play the way they play but I can't.

"Still, nobody's playing the way I'm playing. My style of playing is just... Count Basie said, "You have a significant... All the horn players who have ever been in his orchestra... And these guys are saying, 'You have your own style. They never had nobody play that style of playing, period!' To me it's like, it's original but it's nothing. I know what I'm doing. I just played like I feel.

"They were looking like my movements. 'Keep doing what you're doing," Basie told Reedus. 'Don't worry about your reeding. Just play. You travel on the road with the O'Jays and you learn their music, right?' Basie said to him. And all Reedus could think was, 'I never had no problem, I guess because of my personality. I was always like, we got to do this."

The incident at the Kool Jazz Festival was a defining moment in the life of the Sax Man, though not necessarily the way others came to believe.

First, Reedus played the solo and, according to the musicians who were there, did it brilliantly. It was not just hitting the notes in the right order and with the correct tempo. It was giving the solo style, shaping the music played before and after his saxophone was allowed to soar. The music had a driving force, a power that many musicians would have been unable to achieve and many sax players would have rendered as pedestrian.

Maurice knew he was being justifiably lauded at that moment at the end of their set, yet he also knew the secret he was certain might keep him from ever again achieving such success. He was dyslexic. There were sax players at least as good as he was, as good as he might become, and who could also read music. Have one show up and that would be the end of his career with Sly, Slick & Wicked or any other group with which he might be played. He would be ridiculed. He would be considered a fraud. He would never be as good as his father, he would be disgraced in front of the older man.

The answer, made with the reasoning only possible in an adolescent's thought process, was to never tell anyone he could not read. His mother knew, of course, but she rarely discussed the problem or researched how to help and so she, too, remained silent. His father knew, understood, but could not convince Maurice that if he went to the right college with properly trained musician/professors he would not be ridiculed. He would not fail. He would not learn the way other people do, but he would learn. He would succeed. His condition was not hopeless.

But Maurice could not accept the truth of dyslexia, the truth of his skills, the potential he could unleash with the right assistance. Instead, he told no one except the handful of family members and Cleveland school teachers who already knew, and in the case of the latter, passed him from grade to grade, adding to his sense of inferiority.

It would be 40 years before he had the courage to risk telling a Cleveland based journalist. In that 40 years he had earned the respect of fellow musicians taking a more conventional path to performing. But the 40 years never resulted in his gaining the self-respect he deserved.

Chapter Ten

The Sax Man Speaks

My name is Maurice Reedus, Jr. and I am a street musician; an artist. I started playing in the city... it was 1996. I was downtown and I had no bus fare, and this guy told me to take my horn out and start blowing. And I was a little embarrassed. A little bit. So I started blowing it and these people started dropping in money and I kept on blowing it.

You know I kind of like to save my money to the end of the weekend to pay my bills. But I've been blessed that I've been paying my rent and doing stuff... There's nothing guaranteed.

And then I play with a band sometimes, too. I go out on the road and I play with my father and them, Maurice Reedus, Sr. [The Robert Lockwood All Stars, a group whose longest gig was in Cleveland's Fat Fish Blue until both Lockwood and the elder Reedus passed on.]

110

If I see a bunch of kids I'll play like kids' songs. And then if I see an old couple I'll play something like *I'm In The Mood For Love*, or I'll play something like Tommy Dorsey. There's so many songs they want me to play, and then some people get upset because I can't play them all at the same time. I try to give everyone attention, but it's kind of hard, you know? Play *The Flintstones*, play *The Adams Family*, *The Munsters*, *Andy Griffith*.

I'm a musician. I tell people, I'm a musician. I'm an artist. I'm not a panhandler. Go to New Orleans. Are those people [Buskers—the street musicians] panhandlers? Go to Chicago. Go to Seattle. Got to Boston. Go to Washington. I can name 12 cities right now as we speak that have musicians downtown on every corner. Here in Cleveland I'm the only musician on the street that's consistently out here, and I'm paying my bills! I can't believe that, man. I can't believe I'm paying my bills play- ing on the street, so it can be done. But I never know what I'm going to make. People ask me 'how much you going to make to- day?' and I don't know. I couldn't tell you that because I don't know. It's not about money. You just got to play your horn.

And like my father and Mr. [Robert] Lockwood [Jr.] told me, it takes a strong musician. You've got to have a lot of guts to come out on the street and blow your horn.

—December 21, 2006 Maurice Reedus, Jr., the musician known in Cleveland as the Sax Man, explaining his passion and his life for radio station WCPN Ideastream

. . .

Chapter Eleven

The Sax Takes Him on the Road

I first started to play the saxophone in school in 1967. I joined the band in junior high school. Mostly I was playing by ear. I practiced with my sister and she'd show me the notes. She could read. I couldn't grasp the stuff. I couldn't understand the [written] notes.

"*I was made to love her*," by Stevie Wonder [was the] first song I learned. "Me and Terry [Stubbs] were going to summer school together at John Hay [High School]. That was the summer of '71. He had just gotten with the group—Sly, Slick & Wicked—and they were looking for horn players, and he knew I played the horn. He stayed right around the corner from me, about two blocks from me. He was telling me about this group. He just took me to the rehearsal and John started working with us. John started writing down the horn lines. He would tell me what notes to play.

So long as somebody could tell me what notes to play, I could play the notes. I knew the fingering.

"[Another friend], Marvin Young played both trumpet and trombone. We used to rehearse at the Copa Lounge over on Lee Road. We rehearsed at the Sir Rah House a couple of times. The Funky Broadway. I even set up a rehearsal in the Garden Valley Neighborhood House where I grew up at. We used to rehearse in there a couple of weeks down in the gym on the stage. People used to come in to listen to us rehearse. They'd get a free show.

. . .

"*Surely* was on the charts. This was 1972. The song had been out about a year. We weren't making more money, though. We just had enough money to stay in motels, keep our clothes clean, and eat. We was so hungry, we didn't have no money, we had to split some bubble gum. Eleven guys on two pieces of Bazooka Bubble Gum. We didn't have a cent.

"We broke it up with our hands. You see our manager wasn't with us because he had to leave and go back to New York. We was in our motel rooms, everyone was broke, we didn't have no money. We was waiting for him to bring us some money. We was off then. We had an off day when we weren't working. We had two more days at the motel. The motel was paid so we tried to see if we could get a gig in town until our manager got back.

"We was a show band. I would go out and do a 20 or 25 minute comedy and then go back and the band would play. Then I would come out and announce for the band. One thing about us, we didn't have no money but we dressed like we had money. We dressed sharp. We didn't have a cent, brother. Oh, man, that was so embarrassing. I was having problems with my marriage. I was coming home with no money."

. . .

"I was in the club. I was sitting in the audience and I was boo-ing the band. The police thought I was a drunk and they didn't know it was part of the show. And the police tried to grab my arm and lead me out of the club, but the people said, 'No, he's part of the show. He's the comedian. I would do this thing where I'd walk around and act like I was drunk and I'd sit at a table with somebody from the audience and I'd make all kinds of ruckus. Talkin' all crazy. Lookin' all crazy. And I'm booin' the band and making all sorts of comments to them. Didn't any-body want to hear that shit and like that. The bouncer security came and got me ready to put me out of the club. And there were a couple of times there was people in the audience who was waiting for me to come out because I was talking about them on stage. They got embarrassed, I guess. You know how you have your hecklers? And then you make them look bad in the audience and they get all embarrassed. You know how you can embarrass people? A comedian never gets embarrassed on the stage. No matter what they do, they can't embarrass us but we can embarrass them because they're sitting out there with their people and we're on the stage. It's funny to the peo-ple in the audience. They're not laughing at him [the heckler]. They're laughing at me for listening to him. So it's like he's part of the show.

"If I just say something that closes a person's mouth over it, they won't say something else. That's what gets me in trouble, I guess. I just say something real bad and then everyone in the audience is laughing and this guy burning up, mad. I can't believe he said that to me.

"Then I go over and apologize, and he don't want to hear no apology. I apologize from the stage. Then that whole night the guy's sitting over there burning up and I'm looking at him the whole night while I'm doing my 35 or 40 minute set. And this cat looking at me like he's getting ready to kill me.

"This one guy, the police had to escort me all the way out through the club to my car. They put this guy out of the club, man. This guy was out there waiting for me to come out. His girlfriend's waiting. His girlfriend's trying to get him to calm down, just part of the show. But this guy's drunk and he's just mad because I said something kind of foul. I told him, "I would shut you up permanently but my zipper's stuck." The comment was made while Reedus was tugging at his pants. The crowd went crazy laughing but the heckler couldn't say anything more to him.

The problem Reedus faced was that his act was carefully timed with the music portion and the next show. He couldn't let the heckler keep talking and still finish the act. That's why he decided to say the one joke he knew would stop the man but he didn't expect him to get so enraged.

. . .

"Birdine was staying at my parents' house or her parents' house. All this happened before we got with the O'Jays. They was promoting us. We got off the road and came back to Cleve-

115

land. One of the O'Jays liked Sly, Slick, and Wicked. Walter Williams lead singer for the O'Jays wanted to produce them.

"'[R&B and Soul singer, songwriter] Peabo Bryson, I'm so into you, I don't know what I'm going to do.' Met him down in Huntsville, Alabama. Wanted to be in our band. Guitar player. He was in the dressing room. Started playing and singing. But the singers didn't really want him in the band. The band can't be better than the singers. A couple of years later we see him on Soul Train. He's a big star now. Met the Commodores down South. They were going to Tuskegee University. This was before record Slippery When Wet

"Sly, Slick and Wicked first group I ever went on the road with. I met Terry in summer school in John F. Kennedy High School. He was telling me about this group Sly, Slick & Wicked. He was getting ready to join the group. Charles was Slick. Terry Stubbs was Wicked. I was the first member that they got. Terry was the only one in the band who was allowed to go out and look for musicians."

Maurice was going to Warrensville Heights High School. Terry never heard Maurice play until after he was brought into the band.

"We used to practice in a club at 131st and Broadway—The Funky Broadway. It's now a church. It was a plush club. That was our rehearsal spot during the day. The owner of the club was Ron Carter. I played there before. I did my comedy routines there. Weekends. Thursday through Saturday. At 128th and Miles I did my comedy at the Golden Cocktail Lounge. Opened for a lot of the national acts—The Ohio Players, the Manhattans, the Dramatics, the Staple Singers, Les McCann and Eddie Harris, Gladys Knight and the Pips."

"I made more money doing comedy than I did playing my sax or the Congos. The Road South at 19th and Euclid. Opened for Sam Knight a big promoter in Cleveland. Also had a club on 105th. Brougham Lounge 105th and Euclid. Every club on that stretch I'd do my comedy. O'Neil's show bar."

. . .

"On the road we might play on the door. Sometimes we'd get half the door. Sometimes we'd get all of the door. They'd go for the hotel and we'd go for the door or we'd pay for the hotel and they'd go for the door. Either they'd pay us and we'd pay the hotel, and some places we went to they'd pay for everything. Soon as we'd get into town we'd go straight to the club. Change clothes and stuff in the club. We'd go to the motel after we got some money to pay. Or our manager would go in. We'd sit in the car and our manager would go into the motel and come back with our door key. We never told the manager that there were eleven of us. Sometimes we'd have to sneak someone in the room. Sometimes some of the guys slept in the car if we had to. Or we might get four rooms and two would be on the floor. Or we'd pull mattresses out. All kinds of crazy shit like that.

. . .

"One time we was in a big hotel. We had all these women around us. We got down to Cincinnati. It was like he had everything. We had hotel rooms booked and everything. As soon as we walked in. I couldn't believe it. I was scared, really. We all back in the dressing rooms with all the stars, the first time I was on a big set.

"I met a lot of acts. I carried all sorts of back stage passes but every show I'd walk in with my saxophone and just go back-stage.

"On one tour to Omaha, Nebraska, we was on the stage do-ing a sound check. The O'Jays headlined the show. And New Birth had a song called Wildflower which was #1 for them. Pre-viously the O'Jays had recorded the same song Live in London with Wildflower. It was #1 for them and they had an attitude because they didn't want the O'Jays singing.

"They had a tune out at that time called Dream Merchant that was New Birth and they had their version of Wildflower but next year the O'Jays had theirs but it was written for New Birth. The O'Jays did it after New Birth but it was just live on their album at the Palladium in London. "We did our sound check. But they were there before us—New Birth, but they got an attitude through the whole tour. They weren't hardly speaking to us. They were like street guys, bullying. They got a gun and was demanding their money from the promoter. They got blackballed from the industry. They could sing. They had a good show. But they were like ghetto.

"We were setting up and suddenly everybody started fight-ing. They were choking each other and people throwing stands. I couldn't believe it. They almost knocked down the congas.

"Herb, the conga player, had to move them. We were in downtown Omaha, Nebraska, and no security. It was during the day. There was no need.

"It was like 'Fuck this shit' and 'Fuck the O'Jays' it was crazy and yet we still did the whole tour. They just got an attitude with the O'Jays, period. All because of one song. They were just jealous. New Birth didn't want the O'Jays singing Wildflower.

"Sly, Slick & Wicked [performed] first. Then the Dramatics—we played horn for some of their stuff. Then New Birth, then the Isely Brothers, and then the O'Jays. That's the way it worked. We had the same sound man the O'Jays had.

"We came on time. New Birth was early. We used the same sound system as O'Jays. Sly Slick and Wicked were new/unknown. Same one and the sound guy wouldn't strip it down so New Birth could do it. Lined up. They were just there.

"The O'Jays hang out with their musicians. Sly, Slick & Wicked hang out together. It wasn't like 'I'm the Star.' We even made up skits.

"Me and John would rehearse what he wanted me to say: 'Are you ready for show time? I'd like to bring you, from Paramount Productions, such hits as *Surely* and *Turn On Your Love Lights*, and then I'd bring them up on stage and step back with the band.

"*Surely, Surely, Got to make up your mind.*'"

. . .

"Each time we'd go in to a new town there would be posters on all the poles. It was Sly, Slick, and Wicked's pictures, but we were part of the band. That was very exciting. We were acting like we were stars.

"It was big. It was exciting. We was more concerned about the music, remembering our horn lines, about the music. The people never knew how we felt, but once we really got the show down, it was okay.

"It was exciting to go into a town and see the posters. We felt like stars. Go into a town and we didn't want to leave there. Go into the next town, we didn't want to leave there. Go into the next town. It was cool. I was like, this is the life here. I never wanted it to end. Didn't have to do nothing. Go to sleep in the motel room. Just kick back and look at TV.

. . .

Gladys...augmented

The drug use was not something the younger Reedus liked to discuss because too many assumptions were made by anyone mentioning it. There had been a time in his life, many years earlier, when he had stolen sound equipment from a store catering to musicians, been arrested, and put in a drug treatment program. By his own admission he had been placed in rehab, ironically with Gladys Trice, the first and only female vocalist to be part of one of the first tours by Sly, Slick, & Wicked on which Reedus also performed. When Trice and Reedus first met, Gladys was a highly skilled singer, a woman who had been part of both solo work in church and part of the church choir. The problem she had came from her lack of training and experience in theatrical performance. She was the type of singer who, if you closed your eyes, would seem to lift you with her voice and take you soaring to a higher plane. It was the type of sound greats such as Ella Fitzgerald had achieved.

The problem was that if you opened your eyes to watch her, nothing was happening. She had learned to stand, take the mike, and sing. Nothing else.

Gladys Speaks: "I wouldn't have thought that I'd be in a group that big that early in my career. I used to call home. I

120

used to stay in contact with my mother all the time."

Maurice Again: "We used to do a show before Sly, Slick and Wicked. The band would come out and do two or three numbers and then we'd introduce Gladys. The people down South... the men down south, they was in love with Gladys. Any time you get a lady on the show, on the stage, she would come out and do a whole show, a forty minute show. She'd do it by herself with the band backing her. She'd sing Aretha Franklin songs, Millie Jackson songs, it was like a review. Gladys and Sly, Slick and Wicked. She might have done about two shows a night. It would have came to be about an hour. Two shows a night. The band... we were on the stage all the time.

The band would take a break while I'm out there telling my jokes. Twenty or thirty minutes between every show. When we first hit the stage, the band is playing. The first show for about 35 minutes. Then they would take a break and do my comedy routine. After I got through, Gladys would take the stage. Then Sly, Slick & Wicked would come on. We take a little break 10 or 15 minutes right there.

· · ·

An early time out to serve the country

May 11, 1976. Maurice was 23 years old and unintentionally joined the army.

"Me and my mother went there together [the recruiting office]. We thought it was like a part time job and they was hiring. We didn't know it was the service.

"I was going to get a job. It was on Green Road, the 107 Cavalry. It was the Army National Guard. It didn't say National Guard. It just said part-time work. We were driving by out in Warrensville Heights. We thought it was just a regular job.

"I asked about a job and are they hiring? Then I saw the army uniforms and found out that it was the Army National Guard. But I didn't understand about the Guard back then. It still seemed like a part time job. So I took the test. I don't know how I passed that test.

"There was another guy who took the test with me and we switched names. He didn't want to join. I saw some guy off the street and he agreed to take it. I had him come in with me and had him take the test. His name was Jesse Owens. I never seen him again in my life.

"Once we took the test, he wrote my name on the test and I wrote his name on the form before we turned it in. He printed my name.

"They asked all kinds of questions. They had a little math, about tools, a little yes and no, general knowledge.

"I asked him to take the test for me. I'd pay him some money. He was scared at first, afraid he would get in trouble.

"Actually it was a friend of mine who knew another friend and he did it for twenty bucks. My mother didn't even know I did that that it happened. I never told nobody.

"The guy was paid the twenty bucks and then I found out I passed the test. I was sworn in on May 11 of 1976 and I left like August 11 of 76, left going to Ft. Bragg North Carolina. I stayed there from August until Thanksgiving Day. Graduation was on Thanksgiving Day.

"I did real well in training. Didn't have no problems. My two drill sergeants were from Cleveland. I didn't know that until graduation. Making me do all kind of stuff. Two from Cleveland. Drill Sergeant Hamerick and Hardy (DI—other assistant DI) I didn't know they was from Cleveland until graduation day.

"[I] Played sax on [my] off time. After four weeks of basic. I had more time and playing my horn. I tried to get with the ban on the base but I knew I wasn't going to stay there.

"These guys were already in the army. I used to practice with them. I never did a show with them. I just practiced with them. I had been playing with Sly, Slick and Wicked. This was the middle of the seventies, like 76. I came back home and about once a month we'd have meetings.

"I'd go to summer camp every summer for two weeks. I was in A Troop which is infantry. Then I wanted to get to headquarters H-Company.

"I wanted to be a recruiter, so they sent me to Columbus, to Worthington, Ohio, to go to school to be a recruiter. I went full time. Regular army. How to be a recruiter. How to talk to the guys. Tell them about the Army. Help them fill out the paperwork. And any time I needed any kind of assistance, I had to ask my sergeant. Like when I had them fill out stuff. Tell them how to fill out stuff. I had the high school kids. Talk with them on Career Day.

"I got a Jeep. I used to drive that Jeep all around. Got a couple of gigs with that Jeep. Never had to buy no gas. I drove it up to the Sir Rah House to play a gig. And a lot of people didn't even know I was in the Army.

"I used to be at the office every morning at 7 o'clock, bright and early. I wasn't playing with no band, period. I just went up to the matinees on Saturday and go jamming. Anybody could go in there and play. They had jam sessions like from six to nine. I couldn't go traveling on the road because I had to be a recruiter.

"I was living with a lady then. Her name was Chevonne Johnson. I met her in the summer of 1976. I was with her for a long time. She passed away in 1996 from leukemia. We were together from 1977 to 1983 or 1984. And then we got back together in 1995 before she passed away. But we were always back and forth seeing each other, but we stayed together a long time.

"I was with her the day she died. She went on tour with me down in Florida that summer before she died. She was dying then. Pensacola, Florida with the UAG band. Pat Young arranged that. I took care of Chevonne all the way before she died. Took care of her, fed her, and went to all her appointments with her.

"It was hard for me taking care of her. I know what it is taking care of someone when she's ill. I'd go to band rehearsals then have to come back and check on her. I hated leaving her. Sometimes she'd be all right, sometimes she wasn't. She worked down at the Federal Building. She'd still get up and go to work as a secretary.

"Died September 5, 1996. We had just came from the hospital and I left going to the Indians game (to play). I left her in the house with her mother. When I came back from the game, she was gone.

"We was together all that day, but when I came back from the game, she had died. She was all right all during the day. We was okay. We came back from the hospital, went to get something to eat, she got her jewelry out of lay-away. That jewelry was in the shop. We stopped at this fish place and got a fish sandwich and got back to the house.

"I left going to the game. When I came back, she was dead.

She was gone. Chevonne. I think a lot about her every day. She used to support me and my music. She supported me a lot. And she was with me all during the time I was in the service. Even when I was over in Germany in '78. I was stationed in Wiesbaden. Wiesbaden Air Base. I was over there for about four months.

"When I came back from there, she and me were trying to make some plans. She wanted to go to Atlanta. I wanted to go to California. She had some people in Atlanta so she went out to Atlanta and I went out to San Jose, California where my father was at. She was going to go there and check it out and I was going to check it out, and one thing led to another and she ended up in Atlanta and I ended up in San Jose.

"Each tried to get the other to move but she got a job in Atlanta and he ended in San Jose. That's how they broke up. That was my first time in California. My father was living in San Jose at the time. This was 1979. January of 1979 because I got there just before my birthday. I was just turning 27 then. I was born in 1953.

"I remember when I first got to San Jose at the airport. I had all these winter clothes on. I got into town and I couldn't believe how hot it was. My father had me drive his car and he drove with his girlfriend. They had so much stuff that the police stopped both cars. There had been some break-ins in the neighborhood, and when they seen so much stuff they thought they were doing the break-ins. It was the Mountain View Police. I showed them my driver's license and said I just got into town. I was following my father, Maurice Reedus, Sr.. They thought we were playing games. They had a call someone had broken in and stole some stuff. And they saw the cars and that's why they pulled us over.

"I just started then, 1996. She had seen me playing on the street downtown. She had walked up to me. I was in front of Tower City. That was my main spot, right in front of Tower City, Terminal Tower, I used to stand there all the time. She was on her lunch break and walked by me. I couldn't believe she'd seen me. She used to pick me up at the baseball games. I had just started playing on the street. Then one weekend we drove down to Detroit and I did a game in Detroit. The Indians was playing Detroit. I did real good that day, too, in front of Detroit stadium. Me and her and her mother and her mother's boyfriend, the four of us we all went down there. It had been a while since she'd seen me. It been a good five years. But whenever she and me got together, it was like we never left one another, just right back together.

"Chevonne used to tell her mother off right up. She'd tell her don't say nothing about nothing to him. She know how I was. She knew I didn't take her mother's cell phone. When we came in from the hospital, I picked Chevonne up, carried her upstairs in the house, sit her down in a chair in the living room, got my stuff, got my horn, and went straight away to the game. Her mother was with her. Her mother stayed with her when I was gone. So when did I have time to steal her cell phone?

"When I came back [from the game] there was nobody there at the house. That morning, the first thing she was going to tell me was Chevonne dead, my baby dead, and then she said, I took her cell phone. And I took this and that. Miss Perry she talking about her cell phone, her cigarette case, and I didn't take anything. What are you talking about. I'm tripping on Chevonne being gone, and she's telling me, don't come to the funeral. Don't come to the wake. I didn't go to none of that. Me and Chevonne's clothes was all in that house and I never did get anything. So everything me and Chevonne had together I couldn't get. All of my stuff was up there on the third floor. Everything. All of my suits. All of my shoes. Pictures. Everything. All kinds of stuff. And I used to keep calling and calling and calling. I don't know if she gave it away. It was like my sisters and all them can come to the funeral. My mother can come to the funeral. But I couldn't come. She told my mother and them. They could come but I couldn't come. And I was taking care of Chevonne every day, more than she was. I was making certain she had her medicine at the right time. And I was feeding her and helping her bathe and take a shower. I was doing all of that. [Maurice was with the UAG Band and they were hassling him for being late, for not knowing the horn lines.] They know Chevonne is sick and all that and I've got to be with her. And why was I being late to rehearsals, and I said, well I had to be with Chevonne. They didn't care.

"I was kind of messed up because her (Chevonne's) mother kind of blamed me. During that time, when I first called there because Chevonne's her only daughter and she was all messed up. And she blamed me. She thought I stole her wallet and stole her cell phone. Because I wasn't there when Chevonne died, I lost all my clothes. I lost everything we had in the house together. She wouldn't let me go get any of my things. I lost all my clothes except what I had on that day, that day Chevonne died. And I never did get any of my things I had for years and years. It was like somebody's house catching on fire and you don't have nothing but what you have on. And see, during that time I didn't want to prosecute because I was on probation, and there was a warrant for me already for violating probation. This was the same era—1996—when I was with Judge Gaul. And once again my mother came to my rescue. I didn't have a stitch of clothes except what I had on, an Indians shirt and some blue jeans.

"All she knew was that I was making money (on the street) and she thought that was real cool. And I had just gotten in the paper. That was when Jeff Maynard saw me. I was in the paper. There were a couple of articles done on me. Channel 3, Channel 5, Channel 8, the first time I went out on Ninth and St. Clair I was on all the news by the Erieview Plaza there, on that corner. I was going through a program, too, Fresh Start. I used to go to a lot of NA meetings. Me and Ghani, I used to go to this music store called Sam's Music Shop on Prospect. They had one on the West Side, too. And we knew a friend who worked there, and we was trying to get these modulators to record with. So we went to the store and I knew the guy who worked there. He set out some drum machines for us to pick up (illegally) and what happened was we got caught. In the music store. They were sitting out on the counter. We got out with them. "We was on the west side so we got out with them and had no problem, getting them in the car, and as soon as we started to get back on the freeway to head to the east side, the police pulled us over, and when they pulled us over, there was something wrong with the tags on Ghani's car or something. And then they seen the musical equipment in the car and started asking all types of questions. And they seen the name tags there so one thing led to another and we got arrested and all that. And they got a case—receiving stolen property. So then I had to go to court. This lawyer said we're going to tell this judge that the reason you took this equipment is because you got this drug problem.

"Drug problem? We ain't got a drug problem. That ain't why we stole the equipment.

This is a court appointed lawyer and he said, if you don't tell them that, you're going to go to jail. If I can get you out of this, you can go to a program or something. Even in reality I needed to go to a program but that isn't why I took it. I needed to go to a program, anyway.

The judge who sentenced me—Daniel Gaul—he's like a real good friend of mine. I knew his wife. I met his kids. You don't go before a judge four or five times without going to the penitentiary. He got me sent all the way down to Lorain. I went away to a penitentiary for just about two months. I got shock probation. Then I came back and I had my meetings, and I ended up having another dirty urine. I went before the judge, and Judge Gaul... He knew I'm not no criminal, and finally he said, Maurice, you know what I'm going to do because you're making me look bad in front of my colleagues. Because they know I was on TV a lot and doing this and doing that, you know, with the media and stuff. Good thing the media didn't find out about that. He sent me down to Lorain. I'm going to send you down for one day. They're going to check you in and then release you. I couldn't believe it. I went down to Lorain and they didn't have no paperwork on me. They thought like I was staying there. I told them I'm not staying here. I'm only here for 24 hours. You get to do this paperwork and then I'm going home. And all the POs, all the sheriffs, they thought I was being slick. I got there Thursday and I was supposed to go Friday but they kept me over the weekend. They weren't supposed to. And all of a sudden these attorneys from the state asked me did I want to prosecute the state because they wasn't supposed to keep me.

So they kept me over the weekend. Trying to be funny. I just wanted to go home. Even all the guys I was in there with, they were laughing. They thought I was lying. "You know you're getting ready to go back to the penitentiary. They wanted to cut my hair. "What you want to cut my hair for?" I said, man, I'm getting ready to go home tomorrow. I kept telling I'm not filling out all this paper work. They wanted to give you underwear, give you all this stuff. And I said I'm not staying here. So I just went along with the program. I just sat there. Everyone was filling out paperwork. I didn't fill out nothing. I said, what I am filling it out for. And then when they found out, they let me know they found out, and they kept me there over the weekend, telling me "there's some stuff we've got to check out." But they had no paperwork on me. Then they had to go back to the time I was there before, at the London (Ohio) Penitentiary. You know how they just try to prolong stuff? They just trying to keep me there because I was just so sure I was leaving. And I was sure because I knew what Judge Gaul told me. When he sees me on the street outside the baseball game, him and his wife and kids, he stops and talks with me. If I call the courthouse right now and leave a message for him, he'll call me right back. I even start calling him Danny. Judge Gaul. Different judges from different states hanging out with him downtown. That was in 1998 and 1999. This happened before I met Luwana. I was on probation when she first met me.

"When I was going to prison she moved up to Cleveland, got a job and took care of my apartment for the two months I was away. She moved right on in there when I was locked up. Her and my mother supported me all through that time. They're the only ones that support me with my music right now. Matter of fact almost every horn I've ever had, my mother bought me.

. . .

As Maurice said earlier in the book, the band members who surreptitiously used drugs would often line up and receive cocaine as they went out on stage. This did *not* happen with Sly, Slick, & Wicked because John Wilson did not tolerate such actions. However, it was done with some of the other bands with which Maurice and other among the back-up musicians also performed. And though they would likely be fired if Wilson learned what they had brought with them on the tour, they decided to "help" Gladys "loosen up" without their saying anything to the others.

. . .

Gladys Trice knew she was not bringing the physical showmanship of the other singers to the stage when she sang her set. It was a not unusual problem for many women whose singing was learned in the church where their voices were allowed to soar to great heights but they were expected to stand rather stiffly in the midst of other singers. An audience whose members simply closed their eyes and listened would be entranced, snapping their fingers, bobbing their heads, smiles on their faces. When they opened their eyes, her lack of the choreography that made Sly, Slick, & Wicked so visually appealing hindered her ability to take control of the audience during her set.

Gladys, determined to hold up her end of the show, trusted the Sax Man when he quietly held a couple of different pills from which she was to choose. She knew nothing other than

131

such street names as "Black Beauty" so the choice was a random one. Both were stimulants, though, and they would likely have a similar effect on her performance.

The drug did not get Gladys "high." Instead it lessened her inhibitions. She let herself be transported by the music, her voice, her stage movements, even the way she interacted with the audience so effectively that every man and woman in the place had the impression that Gladys was singing just for them. She created personal choreography on the spot, delighting Fulsom and the band with her ability to swing. This was the Gladys they always knew was inside. This was the Gladys who personally understood how brilliantly she could perform if she just shed her early training to stand still, don't physically call attention to yourself, and sing with a voice that could challenge the angels.

"That was when I knew I would never tour again," Trice explained. "I decided that if I had to get high to put on my best performance, it wasn't worth it." And so, when the tour was over, she went into drug rehab counseling, never looking back except the month when The Sax Man suddenly appeared on her caseload.

"Maurice did everything he was supposed to. He was completely cooperative the entire month I worked with him. But when he had completed his conditions for the court, I know he went back on the drugs."

Today there are acquaintances of Maurice who claim that if he gets a $20 bill he will buy a rock of cocaine. However, Reedus is not an addict any more than the man who has a beer or two before going on stage is a drunk. And asking the same people who are mildly derisive of what they see as typical of a musician who grew old without achieving his dream, none can point to a time they ever saw him buy or use any sort of drug. The handful of times he was hassled by police, he was carrying nothing on him except extra reeds for his sax. And those of us who have been in his homes have never encountered the drugs. If indeed he still uses a recreational substance, he no longer wants it as part of his preparations for a performance. Instead, drugs are a minor part of the mythos known as The Sax Man though Pope seemed certain that they may have been the reason Maurice performed almost entirely on the streets.

"It's sad when you see someone so talented be a slave to certain elements of their life. I've seen Maurice now enough to kind of get an idea of what's really there. And I think the drug habit... it's been killing him a long time."

. . .

The night that changed everything for Maurice's traveling performing life was when he was playing with a band known as The Dynamics. They had a gig at the Sir Rah House where they were welcomed off hours, another local band with skilled teenagers the patrons would enjoy but not yet fully developed professionals.

The Dynamics had auditioned for Harris and were looking forward to being paid for their appearance instead of being forced to do little more than pass the hat or set a tip jar where the audience could reach it. They were thrilled by this new status, excitedly setting up their equipment as they fantasized surprising the audience with the quality of their set's opening number.

And then the equipment failed. "We couldn't get no sound

on the stage and we had to keep the audience occupied," said Maurice. "I just remembered some jokes that I heard my father say, and I started telling the jokes.

" 'Good evening, ladies and gentlemen. It's nice to appear here tonight. [Pause] It's nice to appear anywhere tonight.'

"I was nervous. People started laughing. I didn't think it [the joke about appearing in the club] was funny. I was scared, but people started laughing. And then I told them, 'First of all, I'd like to know if we have any married couples in the house. Do we have any married couples?" Nobody responded so I said, 'Oh, then there's a lot of shackin' and 'packin' going on.'" Suddenly everyone in the audience began laughing. Maurice knew his father would often lead with the [married couples] joke, though he didn't understand it, a common problem for young Reedus who was beginning a career that other comics had been honing for years. "Shackin and packin' were terms that came from a popular song performed by the group Fleetwood Mac. It referred to that time in a relationship when the couple goes a little crazy in bed, having frequent, often wild sex without a subsequent long term commitment.

Maurice continued: "That's the Samsonite [luggage] way. 'Shack up,' I said, and if you don't like it, pack up." I calmed down when the people started laughing. I was okay."

If he wanted to tell more jokes, it was too late. Harris adhered to as strict a schedule for each performance as was possible, a fact that was a great relief for the young Reedus. He had no idea how to segue into other jokes. He wasn't even certain he understood why the audience was laughing so much with the handful he had told. Fortunately there was no time to analyze what had taken place. The equipment came back on and they could start to play. "The first five minutes I kept the people laughing and then I said, 'Okay, people, we got sound now,' and we started the show.

"We were the youngest band the Sir Rah House ever had in its club," Maurice explained. But it wasn't the music that impressed the owner, Robert Harris. It was the brief display of comedy that seemed to hold the audience during a time when other groups might have had problems. "I didn't know you were a comedian," Harris said.

Maurice responded, "I didn't know I was a comedian either."

Harris started laughing, thinking the teenager was joking. Then he asked, "So you going to do this every night? Do your comedy?"

Reedus replied, "Of course." It was as though Harris had been unable to see the talent in front of him, talent that was seemingly far greater than the music. Except...

"All I could think of when I said it was, 'Oh, man, what have I gotten myself into?'"

The rest of the evening was normal. There were seven members of the band, and like everyone else who played at Sir Rah House, they had to audition one afternoon at the club. It was the off time—Monday around noon at the club—ain't nobody around there except the manager and the bar maid, and they liked us. We worked there Tuesday through Sunday from 10 PM to 2 AM six days a week for two weeks. You have Mondays off and that's when they have their auditions. But nothing was ever said about comedy, and had anyone been asked, none of the youths, including Reedus, would have said he knew comedy.

"You did two shows. You did a matinee from four o'clock to eight o'clock, then come back and do a night show from 10 to 2."

The matinees were always free. Bands that wanted to play at the Sir Rah House but had not yet been hired, bands that were playing there or had played there, all might show up for a jam session or to challenge one another. The public knew all this and would come to hear the music.

"We'd play the first set," Maurice explained. "Then the [other] musicians would come up and play the rest of the sets."

Maurice was with Foreign Blue and also played at Sir Rah with Sly, Slick & Wicked. The equipment stopped working right on a Tuesday night, the first of the set. The packed house nights were Thursday, Friday, Saturday, and Sunday.

The comedy. "I just started doing it. I didn't want to just be standing around so I just started talking when the mike wasn't on.

"After the set, we just went home. Then I had to think about the jokes I'm going to do the next night. I got with my father to get some more jokes. I just told Daddy what I did so he started me off with a set of jokes to do."

Ironically it was the comedy that brought the Reedus men, father and son, emotionally closer together. Maurice had not asked his father for help as a musician or as a touring performer. He tried to learn what he heard his father do by remembering the notes, the style, and the phrasing. He tried to be accepted as his father was enjoyed by dressing in the same clothing, smoking the same brand of cigarettes, and imitating his father's posture. By chance he often played the same clubs and other performance venues as his father. But he never sought lessons to improve his horn playing nor took advantage of his brilliance with the congas to more frequently be a part of whatever band his father was in. Instead, it was the comedy that gave them a closeness they had not enjoyed before and seemed never to share again.

Maurice, Sr. did what many stand-up comics did—he collected jokes. He had recordings of comic Redd Foxx. He had various books and packs of 3x5 cards. Whatever he needed to diversify his humor, to separate material that might shock or embarrass from jokes that were for families. He understood the three performances a night when a comic was handling the entire show, not just being a part of a band's revue. There would be an early show that was mostly family oriented. Everyone in the audience was likely to be sober. They were also likely to have the broadest age range.

The second show was also mixed though primarily an older dating crowd. The comedy was part of an evening that would include dinner and, if lucky, the words "It's early. Would you like to come back to my place for a cup of coffee after the show? Or maybe something more?" Sexual innuendo was appropriate for that crowd, and it was not unusual for a couple to return to see the same headliner, this time getting word to his or her dressing room that they had gotten engaged that night and somehow it was the comic that had brought them together.

And the third show, the late night one, had the drunks and the sexual loudmouths. The jokes were often filthy and used *those words.*

The sharing of the knowledge was new to both men. The fear of keeping the commitment to Robert Harris at Sir Rah House kept Maurice, Jr. open to what his father had to say. And the closeness to the time when Maurice would have to be on stage again kept the son intensely fixed on his father's words. And though they apparently never discussed the fact, this was when the secrets of show business were passed from one generation to the next. This was also the moment when Maurice showed his brilliance, his quick mind, his capacity to learn material with greater speed and accuracy than other show business performers who were not dyslexic, who were able to read with understanding.

If either man recognized what was happening that night, what had passed between them, they never said during their myriad interviews for this book. The truth was that Maurice, Jr. was still a big kid. He did what he knew he had to do in order to be able to go back on the stage, but his personal focus was on coolness.

Chapter Twelve

First the Congas, then the Sax

Maurice Reedus, Jr. and his mother went to the music department of downtown Cleveland's Higbee Company Department Store where several instruments were on display. He went directly to the saxophone, checked the reed, clipped the horn to the strap around his neck, and proceeded to blow almost all the wrong notes. In his fantasy he was just like his father, a world class musician with Grammy Awards to his credit and a comedian who worked with the likes of Bill Cosby. In reality he was just another teenager with big dreams, a saxophone he could not play, and a mother who would be making payments that, for many families, would stretch out longer than the child's interest in making music.

· · ·

For the young Maurice Reedus, Jr., a store like Higbee's was a magical place. It was located within the Terminal Tower, once second in height only to New York's Empire State Building and primarily a train station linking Cleveland with the rest of the country. At the end of World War II it handled more passengers than New York's famed Grand Central Station. The lower level of the Terminal, below Higbee's, connected with the luxury Hotel Cleveland [currently a Renaissance] and had a ramp leading to individual shops offering books, Britain's Limited model soldiers and accessories, a fresh fruit and produce stand, and a counter where you could get ice cream, coffee, and sandwiches, among other fare. The department store itself housed the famed Silver Grille, most popular for lunch enjoyed by women dressed in upscale dresses, heels, gloves, hats, and jewelry of often understated elegance.

More elaborate was the sophisticated Fred Harvey's Restaurant located on the Terminal's lower level. It had originally been part of the food system that provided meals served by the Harvey Girls, impeccably trained young single women, to railroad travelers crossing the nation. The restaurant was still part of a layover point for both train crews who had quarters in the Terminal Tower and passengers who briefly stayed in area hotels such as the Hotel Cleveland.

Children such as Maurice learned to limit their expectations of a visit to Higbee's. Music was important in the Cleveland School System and those who wanted to play but could not afford to get a new instrument were given a school owned one to use throughout the semester. Parents with more money took their sons and daughters to Higbee's. The department store was a place to rent or buy the first musical instrument uniquely their own. The department store was also a place where display windows overlooking Euclid and Ontario were transformed into animated displays such as Santa's Workshop where mechanical elves made toys and prepared the sleigh while Santa checked his list. Children from throughout the city stood on the sidewalk, their faces pressed against the glass, entranced by the display and oblivious to the harsh wind coming off Lake Erie. What few understood was that for the parents of Maurice and his friends, the Music Department and the Christmas windows often proscribed the limits of the store where they were welcome.

Helen, a sales clerk in retail fashions who asked that her full name not be used, explained the institutional racism that otherwise permeated the Higbee's experience. "We were taught to stop whatever we were doing and discretely follow Negro families... we were Negro in those days, a few years removed from being colored and a few years before we became black... to watch for shoplifting. The assumption was made that a Negro woman, no matter how well dressed, soft-spoken and polite, fit the profile of a shoplifter. There might be a hundred white women passing through your department, but other than ringing up their purchases or taking their charge-a-plates, we ignored them unless they requested help. The message was that white women didn't steal; Negroes required extra vigilance. None of us ever questioned the directives, but I recall many an instance when one of the store detectives caught white people coming out of the dressing rooms with our clothing being worn under whatever they came in with. We knew this but we never questioned the rules."

Maurice's parents knew there were other rules for shopping in all the downtown department stores for anyone with the audacity to not be white. Black women could not try on any item of clothing including gloves and hats. Somehow a glove being

141

slipped on a white woman's hand to make certain it fit would in no way contaminate it. She could try dozens of pairs, or sit at a counter and place hat after hat on her head as she shopped for new clothes to fit the changing seasons, and other white women would have no qualms about seeing how they looked in the same items.

Let a black woman have the boldness to try on an item of clothing without buying it and the management made certain the clerks understood that item probably had become unsalable. The bigoted hatred was the adult version of pre-pubescent children refusing to touch anyone of the opposite sex because, if they did, they would get "girl cooties" or "boy cooties."

Dining out was also an experience that included subtle restrictions for blacks. One popular chain was notorious for welcoming blacks, seating them with menus and filled water glasses, then having the servers never return to take their order. Requests for service went unanswered, and eventually the family left, their evening ruined.

In the unwritten racial code of Maurice's childhood, any qualified woman could work in a restaurant kitchen whether or not black families were allowed to dine there. Both men and women could often work as janitors, maintenance people, and in the kitchen for clubs on Cleveland's West Side, but in most places only whites could attend the show and spend their money on the entertainment. Blacks were relegated to similar clubs on the East Side.

Downtown Cleveland and the Cuyahoga River became the great divide for workers and entertainment as well. The light rail Rapid Transit was the most blatant example of the city's racism. The original system, built when the Van Sweringen brothers developed the wealthy suburb of Shaker Heights, traveled from downtown to either Warrensville Center or Shaker Green, essentially the edges of the city. The men who rode the convenient system were almost all white, all highly paid for positions in law, management, marketing and the like. The women were mostly black, their stops taking them to the homes they would clean and the employer's children they would care for.

Stand on the underground platform in what was then known as the Terminal Tower and you would see the eastbound train stop long enough to disgorge west side whites making room for black passengers continuing on to the lower income city of East Cleveland that abuts Cleveland itself. East side blacks performed the same dance of bigotry, getting off so that whites could fill the seats of trains traveling west.

Musicians were hired by bars and clubs, with the owners applying the same bias as with other forms of employment. Italian mob owners tended to hire acts with their same ethnic background. Jewish mob owners were the same, as were the Greeks. While the Mafia was popularly presumed to be only Italian, the reality of Cleveland was different. There was the Mayfield Road Gang, for example, a group that fit the Italian stereotype, but it also had the powerful Jewish Combination consisting of a mix of Jewish, Greek, and Italian thugs, extortionists, and corrupt entrepreneurs.

As late as the 1970s the general public did not know what the performers long understood. If you sought your entertainment on the west side of Cleveland, the acts would be mostly white, as would the patrons. If you sought your entertainment on the east side, the acts and patrons would be mostly black. Some people just assumed it was because these were neighborhood clubs so the separation was a result of living patterns.

In truth, it was not unusual for a performer or patron to wander into the wrong club, either seeking a chance to work or a chance to see a particular entertainer, only to be taken outside and beaten.

It was into this environment, one where Maurice, Sr. had spent years fighting for opportunities to show his skills, that the Sax Man first became a part of a kids' band that picked up a few dollars playing for the birthdays and family parties of friends and neighbors. However, his adequate mastery of his instrument did not come easily.

. . .

The young Reedus moved frequently among family members. His parents divorced after his father was caught once too often enjoying the hobby that many entertainers took up when on the road—serial adultery with one or another willing fan. The musicians, singers, and comedians often had some combination of wives, girlfriends, and "dates" that ended in bed with a "What did you say your name was? Well, thanks for the wonderful night."

Maurice, Jr. was not bothered by his father's unfaithfulness. "I just thought he was cool. I wanted to do everything he did."

Maurice continued, "I used to deliberately get in trouble in school whenever my father was in town. I knew he would be the person the principal would call to come to the office. Then I'd show him off. I just thought he was so cool."

Maurice attended Cleveland's Rawlings Junior High where he and his new Higbee's Department Store saxophone were welcomed by the other boys who were playing in the school band and forming groups on their own. It was when he was accepted as part of the latter that his friends faced a problem they had not anticipated with the tall, lanky sax player.

Maurice Reedus, Jr. was dyslexic, a fact he admitted to as few people as possible for almost fifty years. He could neither readily understand the written word nor comprehend the symbols on a sheet of music.

The problems Reedus faced were not unusual and new teaching methods had been devised to help overcome the problem, especially in some of the Montessori System schools. But no one in the Cleveland system discussed what Dyslexia meant or where Maurice might get help. No one familiar with the problem took the time to find him a tutor. There were teachers trained in Special Education who might have provided answers, though again the racism prevalent as he was growing up assured that almost no one would go out of his or her way for this black child whose greatest pleasure was music. Instead Maurice did his best, became the class clown to draw attention away from his limitations, played his sax in every group he could, and was passed from grade to grade without comprehending the work.

Frustrated yet wanting desperately to play in a band like his father, he and some friends created The Dynamics. Talent shows and an occasional kids' party would be their stages, and Maurice was nurtured in ways that let him learn to hear music as others did not, then reproduce it flawlessly. By the time he was traveling the nation as part of the back-up for the successful singing group Sly, Slick & Wicked, Maurice could hold his own with almost any sax player in the country. But it was with The Dynamics that Maurice was nurtured to the next level of musical skill.

"That was hard. I was real slow learning horn parts. But Larry, the guitar player, he was like the leader of the band and he was real smart and knew music really, really well, just like the band teacher. Larry used to work with me and teach me all the horn lines. We'd be on stage doing a show and I'd be like half blowing my part, pretend I was blowing and I wasn't blowing. It was me—I was playing a baritone sax, and a guy named Freddie played tenor sax and Jonathon Smith—Sonny—he played trombone. He's big time now. He's in New York an accountant in New York City.

"He always teases me even when he sees me now—'Maurice, you've come a long way from when you did your one note solos. You're the only guy I knew who did a solo of one note.' "I really couldn't play."

Entr'acte

Other cities cherish their street performers—the girl who towers over the pedestrians as she walks on stilts, roaming among parked cars and excited children as she makes her way from block to block at weekend festivals Or the mime who becomes trapped in an invisible elevator car, bouncing against its invisible walls, desperate for an invisible rescuer to open the door. Or there might be a guitar player who will sing your favorite love song for a dollar or two, a trumpet player, or a drummer. They move among pedestrians on busy summer weekends, their regular presence often promoted to both locals and tourists by area chambers of commerce.

Cleveland has only had one long term busker—The Sax Man, the focus of this book, whose presence on the streets has been measured in years, not weeks or number of ball games. He has amassed fans who seek him out before entering one or another sporting events, one or another theaters, one or another restaurants. And he has repeatedly angered those who see him as a nuisance, an impediment in taking the shortest path to whatever event has brought them to that section of downtown Cleveland. He has been ordered to move by one police officer directing traffic, then welcomed with a smile and salute a block away by a second police officer, also directing traffic but delighted to experience what amounts to a musical interlude letting him briefly escape from the cacophony of automobile horns, slamming car doors, and arguments among couples not fully in agreement about the rest of the evening's entertainment.

Other buskers were of three distinct types. A handful, like Maurice, were competent musicians out to make some money on a sunny weekend afternoon when crowds were moving along the downtown streets. A second group were new to their instrument, new to the musician's hustle. The best that could be said about them was that you didn't flee when you heard them play. Then there were those nowhere near to ready for prime time.

Most painful to remember was the elderly violinist whose concerts outside the Euclid Avenue entrance to the Old Arcade consisted of a careful crafting of each note. The violinist rarely achieved a recognizable song, though the notes were seemingly each on key.

The violinist always dressed in a suit, wore an overcoat, and performed for exactly two hours. He would arrive by car at 11:30 a.m., driven to the arcade entrance by a woman who might have been his granddaughter. The last note would be played almost exactly at 1:30 P.m. Then he would empty his violin case of any money passers-by had tossed in, replace his violin, and return to the car.

Across the street, sitting in a doorway, was a harmonica player. He had the slightly disheveled look of a man in an old prison movie, the character who would sit on the thin, threadbare mattress that passed as his bunk, playing a mournful tune on a harmonica while the rest of the men plotted their return to a free society.

As for The Sax Man, he always seems to be the only street musician who does not see his efforts as a way of supplementing other sources of income. Sometimes, especially during the winter, his horn will have the keys stick so badly on a weekend that he has had to fashion a repair using thick rubber bands until he can get to an open music store. Other street players avoid the harsh cold. But they were playing for free will contributions. The Sax Man saw himself as having a street gig. People were expecting him, they were listening for his music, looking to see what clothes he was wearing. A few, mostly older, mostly having experienced regular encounters for literally the previous several years, had paper money folded in their hands the way someone seeking preferential treatment in an upscale restaurant might palm a $20 bill when greeting the Maître d'. The Sax Man never seemed to notice. He had a concert to give to all his fans.

Near the football stadium, a younger man, skilled as both a song writer and a guitar player/singer, told a story of love and denial to anyone who asked. His brother was in prison in New England where his indeterminate sentence could see him serving life. The guitar player had spent many months trying to gain his brother's release including time spent on the prison payroll where he thought the gift of love and music could somehow earn his brother's release. It was only when he spent lengthy time with his brother following his relocation to Cleveland that he learned the effort to gain his brother's freedom could be   as dangerous for the sibling as whatever sent him to prison in the first place. Details were uncertain but his music reflected the end of his denial and the addition of a melancholic tone underlying his sound.

And in another part of the city was a hustler. He was trained as a barber, cutting hair in his apartment in order to save on such nuisance expenses as rent, licenses, and the like. But his love was the trumpet and he often could be seen on East 9th Street, serenading fans walking to the stadium, the Rock & Roll Hall of Fame and Museum, the Science Center, and the other attractions.

Public Square had a continuously changing group of guitar players with varying skills, including one man who, for two years in a row, played a silent guitar. He wore a high quality suit, perfectly cleaned and pressed, no necktie, frayed heels, and stopped every few feet, strumming the strings and taking a pose that matched the end of a set performed by Elvis Presley in what came to be known as his fat years. Four or five steps, make eye contact with the often confused passers-by, stomp down hard on one foot while running through the notes produced by one hand, acknowledge the invisible applause, then take four or five more steps, turn in the other direction, and repeat.

There were only two consistent, practicing street musicians, and though their backgrounds and skills would seemingly indicate no connection. One was Maurice Reedus, the Sax Man. The other was his somewhat estranged relative by marriage, Kelvin Taylor, a one-legged man better known to passers-by as the Muslim Samad Samad. He adopted for his Muslim faith—Samad Samad. Kelvin took to the saxophone late in life, played with greater dedication than skill, but practiced almost con-

150

stantly either in his apartment or in the shelter of an RTA bus stop. Like The Sax Man, he tried to play for the public every day, though because of his disability he did not risk his instrument or his health in inclement weather.

The unique nature of the city, the transient musical eccentrics, hustlers, and seeming lost souls trying to make a buck for a few days, a week, or a month, meant that the only consistent presence on Cleveland streets for almost 20 years has been The Sax Man. But his story is incomplete without that of his cousin, his father, and the musicians like Blind Eddie Smoot and John "Sly" Wilson who helped him earn his first performance chops. And so the understanding of the life of The Sax Man of Cleveland requires the interweaving of other performers, other times, other places, a unique experience in the world of street musicians and the ways they can enrich the life of a city.

Chapter Thirteen

Traveling Alone Through a Land of Music

There was no musician who filled the same mentoring position for Kelvin Taylor that Eddie Smoot filled for Maurice Reedus, Jr. Instead, he was inadvertently underwriting his training through happenstance as he "earned" one juvenile arrest and another.

Still trying to be a businessman, albeit in the wrong business in the eyes of society, Kelvin made an arrangement to steal a car so it could be stripped, the parts sold individually. Sometimes the men owned their own garage, called a Chop Shop, hired teens like Kelvin and provided a cheap service for dishonest customers who willingly paid less than they would at a legitimate repair business. At other times they moved the parts through a number of different dishonest repair shops. Either way the greatest risk of arrest came with the theft of the car itself—Kelvin's risk. The Cleveland area chop shop with which he made arrangements to bring the car following the theft was comfortable working with a teenager. He had no understanding of the scope of the criminal enterprise with which he was involved. There was also no paperwork, no steal-to-order invoice. The theft would occur in one city, the chop shop would be in a second city, and by the time the owner and/or law enforcement were searching beyond the theft site, the car would be in pieces, each part sold to a different customer.

Chicago was chosen because Kelvin's mother lived there. His father, like Kelvin, lived in Cleveland. The family knew that Kelvin was an entrepreneur but did not become aware that he was involved with crime. And Kelvin felt safe in Chicago because he could claim he was visiting his mother, not moving "hot" merchandise.

Kelvin took a bus to Chicago, planning to drive the stolen car back to Cleveland. But as he stated in the past, he wasn't a very good criminal. He left Chicago and made it part way through Indiana before he was caught. Ultimately he faced a Federal charge because he had traveled through more than one state while engaged in a criminal enterprise. This time he was convicted under the Youthful Offenders Act and sent to the federal reformatory in Milan, Michigan.

"I made it out of Chicago. I got through Indiana." And then the arrest brought the time needed to return to his old love with inmates who shared his interest.

"We would talk about jazz. Like 'Have you heard that artist and our favorite songs, and we would mimic them or what have you. I was the only teenager on the floor. I was housed with the adults.' It was Federal because I took the car across state lines. It was what they call the Dyer Act.

153

"They sentenced me under what was called the Youthful Offenders Act. At that time I was 17 which meant I would get out when I was 21. So they sent me to Milan, and when I got there they had a music room and a music instructor and a jailhouse jazz band. They played for the inmates. They would give talent shows, and oft time they would bring in certain street talent. Professionals who volunteered to come in.

"I don't remember any of them by name, but I was very impressed by this guy who played flugelhorn. He knew all the jazz standards so he was taking requests, and pretty much anything we could call out, pretty much the group knew it."

Kelvin had started trying to learn to play music when he found there was an instrument room in the prison. People donated musical instruments and for the inmates to use while they were there. He decided he wanted to learn to play. "For every day after the work hours, when they called 'Recreation,' we'd go over to the rec hall and there was a room off to the side that was set aside for the music. And there was a quartet there. A guy from Toledo, Ohio, who we called 'Drummer.' He was good, too. He couldn't be more than 17 but he was good, very good. He could have been another Tony Williams (young, brilliant drummer and leader just a few years older than Kelvin). "And there was another brother named Rice. He played the piano. These guys were playing at a professional level, and Mr. Wade... He worked in the Industry in Milan. We made Army beds and lockers for the United States Military. I worked in the Industry, too. I sanded the rough spots off the weldings on the bed and did spot welding.

"But [Mr. Wade] he played tenor saxophone and he was a friend of Stan Getz. He was a really impressive music teacher.

"Now I couldn't even really play, but he said, look, this is all I

154

want you to do. You just blow these two notes here when we get to this phrase.

"I wanted to be a trumpet player, so they issued me a trumpet. Between Rice, Drummer... They had a Fender Bass player that we called "Smut Puppy" because he worked in the prison bakery and always had flour over him, so we called it "smut." He played the Fender Bass, and one day somebody said, "'Go pick up the bass, smut puppy, and let's play the song.' I never will forget the song we were playing [that day] was *Song for My Father* by Horace Silver. And of course there was Mr. Wade on the tenor,

"I practiced but learning was really very, very slow because there really was nobody there to take no time with me. So my father sent me three Rubank Music Books and I worked with them as best as I could.

"We quit work about three o'clock because the count was at four. They have to make sure all the bodies are accounted for. And then after that we stayed in for the dinner call, and after dinner they had another count. You go back to your cell for the four o'clock count.

"The guitar players could take their instruments into their cells because they were quiet and wouldn't disturb anyone— things like harmonicas, guitars, melodicas—what they call C-melody instruments. A melodica is really like a breath operated piano. You blew into it and it has little keys for changing the notes. But the horns were kept in the rec room, probably to keep down any complaints about the sound and to prevent the heavy instrument from being used as a weapon.

"We stayed in the dorm until 5 when we got up for dinner. After dinner you go back to the cell block for another count which is to about 6 o'clock. When the six o'clock count is clear, it's rec hour. You can walk the yard. You can go over to the rec room where they had Ping-Pong, pool, rap sessions... "Each kind of criminal hangs with his own kind—con men with con men. I hung with the musicians. We would go in the music room and I would listen to them. I would be off in another little sub room trying to work out the trumpet. So what happened was a guy was maybe a level or two above me. He was learning alto sax while I was learning trumpet. He starts showing me the fundamentals to reading, and then after I got the fundamentals on, on down time that's what I did. I would stay on what I called my music theory—learning all the paper work, how to read, the various breaks, the various notes, the various timings.

"They would let me keep the mouthpiece, and you have what you call buzzing. You take the mouthpiece to build up your lips. You got two types of buzzing. You got one where you just buzz with your lips. What that does is limbering up your lip.

"Trumpet is an instrument... not like other instruments where the longer you play, the stronger you get. Trumpet is an instrument where you play to a point and when your mouth gets tired, you stop and rest. It's like lifting weights. Your body have to absorb the exercises and the forms that you put upon it.

"That's what happened to Louis Armstrong in Europe. His manager was pushing him so hard because he could hit 70 high Cs one after another. They was pushing him so hard his mouth burst open and he had to lay off that whole year. He never did actually recover from that. He always had a problem with that for the rest of his life. That also happened to Freddy Hubbard so they tell you, you practice to a point and then you stop and rest for as long as you practice.

"There was a work strike in Milan and I was indicated in it. At that time I had heard that the work strike was coming so I got out of the Industry and became a dormitory cleaner. But for whatever reason I got hung up in it and they shipped me out to El Reno, Oklahoma.

"When I was in Industry we got fifty cents an hour and three days good time per month if you worked in the Industry. But on my tour out to El Reno we went through Terre Haute, Leavenworth, Texarkana on a bus. It took us about a week when you got done with all the stopovers because we stayed two weeks in Leavenworth. The bus came and got us and we went down into Texarkana, Texas, and from Texarkana, Texas, we made it out to El Reno. There they had a music program, too. I was issued a trumpet. It was the same thing. I would go during Rec time. I would go there but I didn't have nobody but myself, and along with that I couldn't make no progress because by me being a Black Muslim, we had the jacket of being troublemakers.

"There was always a conflict between me and the guards, me and the guards. And they was always put me in the hole, so every time they put me in the hole I got behind in my music practice. I was with Elijah Muhammad. I joined. Malcolm X had been assassinated by the time I came in about 1963 or 1964. He hadn't been long assassinated when I joined because I remember that it was still the big talk t h e n .

"Out there in Oklahoma there was always some conflict like they mysteriously found a shank in my cell, and off to the hole. You go to a little court and I said, Man, you know Muslims, we don't carry weapons, so why are you going to lay there and give me this case like that. I'm gone for two weeks. I can't practice music. I couldn't buzz with the mouthpiece because they took that away, so the most I could do was music reading. I kept up with my music reading and my theory.

"The hole... segregation is actually what they call it... For want of a better term we call it a three in one system. You got your

157

toilet. You got your bed. You got your sink. And if you're still incorrigible they take you out to a strip cell where they give you a mattress to go to sleep on. The rest of the time you just sit in your cell and you sit on the toilet and they let you out every third day to take a shower. You don't smoke. You don't really get no daylight because it's a barred gate, then there's a little space with another door, and in that door where he can come and look at you. So if you're still giving you problems, they take you down this hallway where you got this door and you got the real hole with nothing. It's off to the side and it's kind of inside a little wall and they lock you in there. They feed you on a paper plate. You don't come out. You don't talk. You don't see nobody. Old Nellie. That was the name of it. They ask where you are and if the person says they took him to Old Nellie that means you've exhausted the other two means of segregation and they done took you to Little Nellie, the hole in the wall.

"All throughout the prison system, the primary thing is to get out. You can't get out if you're making trouble.

"You had agitators—guards and inmates alike. You got guards that are more agitators than inmates. It's something for them to do.

"I had to contend with that. That's another reason why I couldn't make any forward progress like I wanted when I was incarcerated.

"In any rate, I got out in 1971 and I was paroled to Chicago, and at this time there I had more or less left music alone other than just listening to it. I was 21. My mother and my cousins, they lived in Chicago. You see my mother passed while I was incarcerated and I had six months left on my sentence and they were debating whether they should let me go to the funeral. So they decided and when I came back, they gave me a job working outside the prison on the farm. I worked in the slaughter house. We would skin cattle for the prison, and that's what I did until I did my last day and was released. I reported to Muhammad's Temple.

"When I got to Chicago, the Nation of Islam owned a lamb slaughter house, and I told them that's what I did when I was incarcerated and I got me a job there. Learning how to dress out live cattle... lambs.

"I was pretty much just into being a Muslim, going to work, praying, selling papers, selling fish, listening to jazz. That was pretty much my life, so that's what I did until I came back to Cleveland. I have family here in Cleveland—my two brothers, my grandmother, my aunt... because I was born and raised in Cleveland so I resumed a life here.

"I opened up a jewelry store making jewelry out of nickel, copper, and brass on E. 116th and Buckeye. I made jewelry and I sold jewelry, incense, oils, and jewelry.

"I learned to make jewelry in Chicago, before I left Chicago. I studied with the Hebrews when I was in Chicago. You see, at first I used to just sell the jewelry. I used to go to the wholesale house and buy it wholesale and take it out in my earring case and go through the streets of Chicago selling it—earrings, cigarette lighters, incense. That's what I did, and back during the 80s it was a gold mine. A guy could really take care of himself.

"And when I came back to Cleveland, I brought those skills with me." "I learned to make jewelry from the Hebrew brothers. Earrings and bracelets out of brass. And a brother I knew who was in the organization Yahweh Ben Yahweh (The leader of a group that considered themselves the lost nation of Hebrews.) They were jewelry makers like no other, and the ones that went back to Israel for a while, that's what they did. They

159

made jewelry and sold it to tourists. So a brother I knew who was in the organization, I saw him on the bus one day, and when I was selling costume jewelry, I used to take him with me and he told me, "Man, I can return the favor now. We got a little shop on 79th and Clyde in Chicago so I went by and he started showing me the ropes, how to make jewelry, supply stores, the metal shops where we buy the metal, and then I cultivated it, started adding my own touch.

"You see, when I got into music I left all that because the music sustains me."

Chapter Fourteen

The Reeduses Again in the Beginning
There was the Father

To see Maurice Reedus, Sr. standing face-to-face with Maurice Reedus, Jr. on the stage of Fat Fish Blue, the older man's last steady gig with the Cleveland based Robert Lockwood, Jr. All Stars, was like observing a variation of a fun house mirror on a carnival midway. Their height was the same. Their weight was the same. Their facial structures were identical. Each wore a beret. Each wore clothing that seemed reminiscent of one of the Beat Generation coffee houses that flourished beginning after the Korean War. Each held his horn with one hand, his fingers snapping to the beat with the other.

Maurice, Sr. had arrived with the band, the group playing their first set when, unexpectedly, Maurice, Jr. quietly entered the restaurant, leaving his winter clothes and his saxophone case wedged behind the bandstand. He made his way to where

Robert Lockwood Jr., 91 years old and unknowing he was days from death, sat apart from the elevated stage, his guitar at his side, his body sagging slightly as though he needed to conserve as much energy as possible in order to climb to the stage to begin his performance.

Maurice, Jr. took the aged Lockwood's hand, held it for a moment, spoke briefly, and then walked to the stage where his father and the other musicians had made a place for him.

The restaurant was packed, the servers having a difficult time moving among the men and women who ate and drank while awaiting the performance of the legendary, Grammy Award Winning blues guitarist.

The evening's entertainment, with the exception of the presence of the Sax Man, was typical of downtown Cleveland nightspots. Some had high cover or admission prices when nationally known and world class acts were playing. Others might have only a tip jar in which folding money was dropped to show appreciation, the food and liquor prices on the menu no different than any other night. For reasons never quite understood, Cleveland had become a music town where performers seemed to appear at different venues unrelated to their skills and fame. Lockwood and his All Stars, men who had traveled the world to great acclaim, played for a fee that amounted to little more than might be achieved with a free will offering.

The younger Reedus climbed onto the bandstand and stood quietly as the All Stars finished a Cab Calloway number. He was almost sixty, his father two decades older. He seemed slightly tense, holding his sax as though the keys might accidentally open, the notes he had hoped to send soaring skyward instead falling to the stage floor in disharmony. He seemed to have become most comfortable, not with the jazz classics but with the music of his childhood, the theme songs for after school and weekend cartoon shows, and the solo he had performed more than two decades earlier but still used as his signature adult piece.

Clevelanders often had a more narrow awareness, thinking of the Sax Man as performing the music of the streets. Audiences leaving one or another of the Playhouse Square theaters would encounter the younger Reedus playing the final musical number of the show they had just seen performed. They did not know that the theater ushers let Reedus come inside as the show was coming to an end. He would listen to the final music, go outside, and start playing as the exit doors opened. It would be the same song they had just heard, a continuation of the theatrical experience, and many people responded with a tip. But this was Fat Fish Blue, a restaurant packed with Lockwood fans who seemingly had no interest in hearing The Sax Man.

Maurice, Sr. held his horn with a lighter grip than that of his son, the sax an extension of his fingers. His was the background of the be-bop generation, of Charlie Parker, Duke Ellington, and Ella Fitzgerald, of a world where everyone who mattered was a "cat," and if you forgot the words to a song, you would substitute sounds for lyrics and "scat." He could play seemingly anything because he turned professional at a time when survival meant everything from being the only black musician at a Bar Mitzvah Party to polkas for a Polish wedding to backing the biggest names in show business when they needed a horn for a recording session. You were versatile and ate or rigid and starved.

Both Reedus men were smokers, their fingers stained by nicotine. Both men recalled past triumphs, the Sax Man validly fixated on the 1975 Jazz Festival, his father still looking ahead to the next triumph that might be his.

. . .

It was hard to tell what first caught the attention of the customers waiting for the All Stars to finish their set and Lockwood to
make his way onto the stage to sit and play alongside them. It
is doubtful that anyone recognized the Sax Man. The room was
too dark, his entrance too quiet, the show not one where he
would be introduced before playing. All that is certain was that
unlike the other musicians, The Sax Man did not play for the
entertainment of the paying customers. Instead he blew his
horn for the most important audience he knew, an audience of
one, his father. The two men, physically so alike, seemed to be
from another era, a time the older man knew well, the younger
would never directly experience. Cleveland had been a college
town in the late 1950s and early 1960s. Case Tech, Western Re-
serve University, Cleveland College, Cleveland Institute of Art,
Cleveland Institute of Music... so many schools all clustered in
the area that was called University Circle for obvious reasons.
Students and younger faculty members, newly graduated nurses from the Frances Payne Bolton School of Nursing, and in-
terns starting the most exhausting portion of the last years of
their medical training all lived in aging and often disreputable
apartments. Their lives were filled with endless studies and
field work, their only escape coming from the myriad small
clubs and cheap restaurants, many of which offered music in
addition to food.

The locations were what might be called "pseudo-Bohemi-
an." The young women dressed mostly in black—black sweat-

ers or blouses, black slacks, black berets, and only their rich red lipsticks varied the mono-color scheme. Most smoked imported cigarettes, not necessarily knowing the taste difference between a pack of American Lucky Strikes and the French Gauloises they claimed to prefer. A few rolled their own using a small pouch of tobacco and a pack of Zig-Zag papers. Sometimes they made what amounted to a cheap cigarette. At other times their creation gave off the unmistakable aroma of pot, a cross between what you experience when a skunk passes by and holding several crayons under your nose. Given enough patrons enjoying such an experience and the smoke would give a mellow high to everyone in the coffee shop, including the performers.

. . .

That was then; the Fat Fish Blue appearance was now. Musicians who knew both men suspected that there was unspoken jealousy though they were hard pressed to explain why or how. Some thought that Maurice Jr. so idolized his father that when he realized he might be the superior musician, he deliberately tried to fail. Others thought Maurice Sr. was jealous of his son's superior talent, that he might have been concerned that his son would reveal superior musicianship when they were heard together. Still others just claimed that the father was a consistently professional musician, putting in the hours of practice needed to excel in performance, while the son was too lazy to practice adequately and thus too erratic to play effectively with a top professional band. That night they stood together, the father playing the song, the son playing a solo riff.

165

The Sax Man seemed to channel past triumphs, the unexpected call for a solo causing him to unleash the brief but explosive music that had helped earn a standing ovation at the 1975 Kool Jazz Festival. It was a performance at once familiar and fresh to the ears, like the theme song of a jazz group from the Big Band era when music that had been played a thousand times before had to excite an often jaded fan base. And when The Sax Man had finished his solo on the small restaurant stage, his father and the other musicians moved back to the front and finished the song with him.

. . .

The Sax Man seemed not to hear the audience response to his solo on the stage of the restaurant. He apparently never registered the intense applause, never noticed that when Robert Lockwood, Jr. slowly made his way onto the stage, the men and women seated at tables or standing, holding drinks, waiting for an opening to sit down, had been momentarily distracted by the brilliance they had just heard. He did not see his father's reaction or the looks of the other All Stars.

The younger Reedus was focused on the familiar. There was a basketball game in progress in the Quicken Loans Arena that night. Earlier in the evening, after the fans had gone inside to watch the Cleveland Cavaliers play whichever rival basketball team was in town, he had walked to Fat Fish Blue where he had just dazzled a restaurant filled with another musician's fans. Then, instead of playing an encore, he stayed focused on the streets. The game would be ending soon. He needed to play for the fans while they were leaving.

Not that Maurice was on anyone's payroll. Fat Fish Blue contracted with Robert Lockwood, Jr. and the All Stars. The Quicken Loans Arena contracted with no one. The band stand at Fat Fish Blue had a tip jar to one side for anyone who wanted to say an extra thank you to the musicians. Maurice had his empty case open for tips as he played. There were no expectations at either place, no obligations.

But the Sax Man was committed to the streets, whether or not they wanted him, whether or not they welcomed him, whether or not they heard him over the din of cars and car horns, busses and police officers bellowing to be heard over the traffic they directed. Reality did not matter. He was the Sax Man and they were his fans. They expected to see him, regardless of the hour. His public expected to hear the sound of his horn and would feel their downtown experience to be was lessened by his absence, whether outside a sporting event, a Broadway company on tour, or a cluster of nightclubs and restaurants on East 4th Street, the Warehouse District, or other location. Such was the driving force whenever he went out to perform. Maybe it was even true.

Chapter Fifteen

Relationships

A meaningful adult relationship seemed difficult for the Reeduses, father and son. Neither seemed certain how the other felt about The Sax Man's unusual approach to earning a living on the streets. And under the best of circumstances, when each man was playing a gig in a part of the country where the other had also appeared, there was still difficulty with communication. For example, there was the night that the Robert Lockwood All Stars played at Severance Hall, the home of the world famous Cleveland Orchestra.

The Sax Man was welcome to come into Severance Hall and be a part of the audience. This was a performance venue few musicians ever have a chance to experience, and Maurice Reedus, Sr. would have been proud to have his son watching and listening to him on such a stage. Instead, the Sax Man arrived at Severance Hall, but did not go inside. Instead, when the show was over, the police directing the departing audience as their cars merged with the evening traffic on Euclid Avenue, the older Reedus and his fellow musicians left by way of the performers' entrance. And as they headed for their own cars, they saw The Sax Man standing under the harsh illumination of a street light, blowing his sax with the skill and intensity of that day at the Jazz festival. .

Was the action a joke? An in-your-face challenge or rebuke by the Sax Man to his father? An action neither man understood? The elder Reedus is dead. The younger man is not given to introspection.

. . .

The older Reedus had been both a part of that post-war world of hippies and players, and a step removed. He was dealing with all the problems of divorce, with small children who were upset by change in the family's living arrangements, and by the vagaries of adult romance. He had to regularly seek day jobs to pay the bills while trying to increase his playing gigs in nightclubs, restaurants, bars, and music festivals. He had mastered pop and bebop, jazz and blues. All he wanted was enough money to get by as he worked to constantly improve his music and regularly hook-up with some of the great performers of the day.

Clubs after the Korean War:

The life of a post-Korean War era musician was not one the Sax Man, still a little boy in elementary school, could comprehend. The older Reedus, working to make a reputation as both a stand-up comedian and a saxophone player, traveled the country playing clubs, festivals, and private parties. His music could be heard on recordings, sometimes as part of a band, sometimes backing one or another singer. It was a time when radio stations still introduced new recordings and re-cord stores had listening areas where you could hear the music before buying. Promoters went from station to station, some-times bringing the musicians for an interview or even an im-promptu session in the broadcast booth.

Maurice Reedus, Sr. quickly learned that the life of a profes-sional musician trying to move higher in the business demand-ed versatility and a willingness to travel. He played R&B, Jazz, Pop, and anything else people would pay to hear. He worked in clubs, for private parties, and as a studio musician backing famous singers making their latest records. The only problem, one he shared with previous generations of musicians, was getting paid. The club owners lived in the cities where Ree-dus and others played, sometimes for a night or weekend, but rarely for longer than two weeks before moving on to the next gig. The club owners shopped in local stores, sent their chil-dren to local schools, and contributed to local charities. The musicians had no such ties, and if there was a dispute over pay, the local businessman/club owner would always be favored over itinerant musicians.

Typical of the elder Reedus's problems, one his son would later share, was to go to a club where he and the band in which he was playing were scheduled to appear. The equipment would be set up and a sound check made. Then they would go to wherever they were staying—a hotel if one rented to blacks, a private home if the racism of the city denied them access to normal accommodations.

The show would take place as advertised in the club, on fly-ers posted around the city, and on the radio if there was a local station that featured what was then called "race music"—R&B and the like. Often there would be a sold out crowd, and if the band had a manager watching the entrance, a count would be taken to see how much the house had earned. It would be late when the band packed up their instruments and prepared to return to wherever they were staying to get a few hours' sleep before driving to the next gig that might be in the next state.

If all went as agreed upon, the manager would go to the club owner immediately after the last show. The money would have been counted and whatever cash payment had been agreed upon—flat fee, percentage of the house, etc.—set aside. That was when a crooked club owner would explain that he was exhausted and he was certain the musicians must be as well. The money was safely locked away, so why not get some sleep, and then meet first thing in the morning, the band being paid just before they rolled out of town.

The problem came when the manager went back to the club at the agreed upon time. A crooked club owner would be gone, the building locked tight, and no one at the hotel would know where he could be found. During Maurice, Sr.'s coming of age experiences with not getting paid, there was little recourse. If the city was large enough for a Musician's Union, a representative might talk with the club owner. Often the clubs were owned by men who were at least on the fringes of organized crime in their community. Such men did not yield to what little pressure could be applied on behalf of the band. The result was that promised assistance rarely, if ever, occurred. Instead the business agents took dues from all the musicians without regard to race, religion, or politics. Then the musicians' union leaders booked the musicians as they saw fit, set pay as they chose, and answered to none of the members.

. . .

I didn't get out there [touring clubs] until the Korean War from 1955 to now. [The segregation was such] James Brown never played in an auditorium where the blacks couldn't come in, the elder Reedus explained. His contemporaries were performers like Nat Cole, a brilliant piano player who became a singer only after he was told that club dates would be ended if he only played the piano.

. . .

The elder Reedus was a tall man, lean and urbane in dress and actions. His skills with a saxophone had taken him around the world, including three extended trips to Japan.
Under the best of circumstances his career choice made him almost a magical stranger to his oldest son. There were gigs in Cleveland, more work and more money in other cities. He gained a modicum of fame, especially among other musicians and stand-up comics, and his urbane image on the bandstand brought him attractive women only too willing to share his bed for a night or however long he might be in town.

Divorce was a given for a performer like Maurice, Sr. It was the rare man who admitted he was lonely on the road, rarer still when someone like singer Al Martino insisted that his wife come with him wherever he performed so he was certain to remain faithful.

Maurice, Jr. understood little of this. He witnessed his mother's anger towards his father without seeing the numerous sexual affairs that were emotionally devastating for her. All he saw was the way strangers reacted to his father's saxophone, to his father's jokes, to his father.

"I thought he was so cool," explained Maurice, Jr. "I just thought he was the coolest man I knew." And though the son wanted to be just like his father, he rarely if ever talked in-depth about the music, the road, the groupies, the relationship with the older man's first wife, and how much he idolized the older man. He also never explained how he could take great delight in making enough of a class nuisance of himself that his high school principal felt the need to summon both Reedus, Jr. and senior to his office.

. . .

The older Reedus was not a man to involve himself in his son's world. When the school had Career Day and a parent would come to class, none of them were nightclub performers. None of them could talk about the world of show business the way the elder Reedus was able to do. But even the coolest of parents had to show up at the Career Day assemblies for the other kids to appreciate him, and that wasn't possible for someone who was either on the road or working most of the night.

The answer for the Sax Man was to regularly screw up during his classes. He knew his mother's job was such that she could not leave work unexpectedly for anything short of a medical emergency. That was why they listed her estranged husband as the first person to call when Maurice, Jr. was being a discipline problem.

Maurice, Jr. came to understood that while his father probably would not show up for a school program, he would come by when his son was acting out. He deliberately misbehaved as often as he thought he could get away with it without finding himself in serious trouble. And each time Maurice, Jr. would be sent to the principal's office where the principal's secretary would call the elder Reedus to come to school for a conference with the principal.

The calls delighted the youth who knew his father would dutifully show up, learn what transgressions of the school rules his son had committed, and either approve an in-school punishment such as detention or promise to punish him at home. Either way, Maurice, Jr. would make certain he and his father walked the long way from the parking lot entrance to the school through the halls to the principal's office, passing the maximum number of fellow students. He wanted them to notice how the older man dressed, held himself, held the cigarette he was likely to be smoking in those days before building smoking bans. "He was just so cool! I wanted to be just like him."

. . .

The Sax Man's father was fortunate during his days as an itinerant musician. He never got hooked on drugs, and though he began drinking so heavily that it endangered his health, he had the strength to stop when the doctors treating him at the Veterans' Administration (VA) Hospitals helped him understand his future was tied up in his willingness to give up alcohol. Ultimately he was able to perform until less than a week before his death at a much older age than he once expected to live.

. . .

The Sax Man never realized that many of his on-the-road experiences were no different from what his father encountered a generation earlier, and the elder Reedus learned from the musicians who had gone before him. The differences were not in the relationships that evolved, the broken marriages and the hushed trips to any doctor who could write a prescription for penicillin. Instead they were in the racial tensions that still lingered as Maurice Reedus, Sr. was able to leave the military, focus on his sax, and take fewer and fewer day jobs between band engagements.

. . .

"I didn't get out there [playing the saxophone professionally] until the Korean War from 1955 to now [The Sax Man's father died August 22, 2008]. James Brown and Nat Cole they had separate audiences and all that junk. James Brown, he was never playing in an auditorium where the blacks couldn't come in. Then you had that prejudice type thing and the union never did anything for you. They say they would, only what did they do? You pay your dues, and they used to come around in Cleveland and I wasn't making any money at the time. I was making $10, $11, $12 and they'd come around and take $2 or $3 and call it band dues. We tried to dodge that cat. But they never got you any jobs, not blacks, anyway. Acts came into town, they'd

175

hire the white cats to play behind the acts.

"I remember once when we had our dues paid up and we went to play a club called the Ritz in Youngstown at the theater, but I guess the mob had that because we played there a week of New Year's and Christmas. It was weekends on the front and on the back. And the cat said, 'Well, you finish on a Sunday. Come back on Monday and get your money.' So we come back on Monday and a padlock was on the thing. A padlock. So we talked with the union and the union said, 'we'll look into it,' and those folks were supposed to get you your money. We never heard from them again."

The union rep would get a contract with a club, collect the money for the musicians who were sent there to play, then receive more money under the table. Depending upon the group, the union rep, and other factors, there could be as much as half the money being paid for the musicians actually going to them. Sometimes a band leader would get an envelope of cash apart from the money paid to the band under the contract. Sometimes the union rep would cut a deal where a relatively small amount of money was paid to the musicians and at least as large a sum was divided among the rep, the band leader, and the club owner.

"[Radio personality] Joe Finan had dances. Bring in Della Reese, Dinah Washington. And we'd play behind them while the kids danced. We'd never get paid for that. They called it 'exposure.' Wasn't nobody hiring us or even hearing us. It's not in the stores. It's not on the air and generally, when you get the record going, they give you maybe $50 or $60 to cut the record.

"I remember when Nat Cole and I think Frank Sinatra at that time were getting five cents a record, and if you weren't that high, you'd get a penny a record. Nat made that company—Capitol Records—profitable. "Nat was a piano player. He was in a joint and one of the cats told him to sing or they'd fire him. That's when he did that number *Sweet Lorraine*, though he didn't know all of the words. He had two trios—the Nat King Cole Trio with Oscar Moore and then they had the Charles Brown trio and Oscar Moore's brother played guitar for Charles Brown. That's when we were down around King Records in Cincinnati.

"It was just a huge thing. They said find something you really like to do, you'll never have to work again. It won't be like work then. It will be fun. We had fun. We didn't make no money. It was doing drugs and being on the road. Cats was dying young. Then when you get something big, like I did something with Lionel Hampton around 1969. His wife, Gladys, she was the boss. 'Oh, you're playing with Hamp? Oh, I'll give you this here. You'll get yours because you're playing with Hamp now.' "You got cheated all the way around because nobody had nothing, and the ones who had it was cheating the ones they were hiring so they give them just a little bit.

"It was a rough road. I remember once when I was playing over here and there were no blacks playing on the west side at that time—it was like '56 or '57. I was playing... the band was white. I was the only non-white dude. We was playing around 54th and Lorain. The music was good, and I was telling jokes, too, at the time. There was no cussin' in the jokes. The jokes were all clean. Jokes you had to think to get the answer.

"One time somebody stood up in the back and said, 'you can't tell that kind of jokes with white girls in here.' 'Or you're losing your mind.' The joint was packed and the guy was causing trouble so the owner and his wife jumped over the bar and started knocking him out. They were making money so they weren't going to let him act like that.

"He [the bar owner] had a billy club like the cops had. She [his wife] just had a fist and a towel in her hand.

"I was tellin' jokes like that. They were clean like Redd Foxx did on his records. There wasn't any cussing. They were clean. Like I said, 'There's this fellow that went to this house of ill repute. He didn't have no arms and no legs. And he knocked on the door and the lady come to the door and he said, 'I know what kind of house this is.'

She said, 'You got no arms and no legs. What can you do?'

He said, 'I rang the doorbell, didn't I?'

Another part of the comedy included poetry such as: 'There ain't no justice in this whole land. Not since my sister got a divorce from her old man. I had to laugh at the judge's decision. They gave him the kids and they weren't even his'n.'

"I'd say, 'What's the difference between meat and fish? You're not supposed to beat your fish.'

"You had to think."

"Me and the organ player used to play at a place called Memories on Brecksville. You come off of I-480 or right around the corner from the vets' hospital. We occasionally play there as a dual.

"Most of the people like us but there's still some idiot somewhere. Like we were playing there two or three weeks ago and two cats back there were sitting, talking to each other. I know they've been there before because we'd seen them there before, so I think they were maybe friends of the bartender or friends of one or two of the bar girls who work there. "All of a sudden the joint got quiet for a minute and one of them said, 'Nigger!' real loud, and everybody heard it. Nobody else say anything. And one of the girls said, 'No! No! Take it outside.' They were probably talking to each other about something else, but at the time it came out, things just happened to be quiet, and I thought... 'Oh, boy...' And that's what it's like today, but a whole lot better. You know, a newer generation.

"I was saying some jokes before and they wouldn't like I was doing them. We was talking about color in some kind of way. I would say, like, 'My parents were mixed. I don't know which side to hate.'

" 'It's hard when your parents are mixed because you wake up in the morning with the taste in your mouth of filet mignon and biscuits. Pheasant and black eyed peas.'

"I don't care what color you are. When it comes to going to bed and turning out the light, it becomes a question of who washed.

"You get it in through your comedy because it takes the truth to tell a joke.

"'What's the difference between a joke and a wise crack? A joke is a woman who has ten kids and a wise crack is a woman who has none.'

"You have to think. It might be too much for you."

And for Reedus–Senior and Junior–there was always the money:

The Sax Man: On the road we might play on the door. Sometimes we'd get half the door. Sometimes we'd get all of the door. They'd go for the hotel and we'd go for the door or we'd pay for the hotel and they'd go for the door. Either they'd pay us and we'd pay the hotel, and some places we went to they'd pay for everything. Soon as we'd get into town we'd go straight to the club. Change clothes and stuff in the club. We'd go to the motel after we got some money to pay. Or our manager would go in. We'd sit in the car and our manager would go into the motel and come back with our door key. We never told the manager that there were eleven of us. Sometimes we'd have to sneak someone in the room. Sometimes some of the guys slept in the car if we had to. Or we might get four rooms and two would be on the floor. Or we'd pull mattresses out. All kinds of crazy shit like that.

But when he started:

Marla, a waitress in the Tucson, Arizona, restaurant known as the Black Watch (Home to the "world famous Kiltie Burger," according to the sign on the outside wall.), was pretty, intelligent, compassionate, and a hard worker. Placed in the historic context of the region, she had the qualities that a century earlier worked for Fred Harvey when he hired such young women as waitresses and tour guides for wealthy businessmen and vacationing couples going to the Grand Canyon.

The waitress could easily have worked in any field she desired, a fact that frequently led new customers to ask why she was in a minimum wage job many people thought demeaning. She explained that no matter what her life was like, working as a server gave her hope. Every day she went home with money in her pocket. And if the monthly bills had come, she also knew she would have money to meet her obligations. There would be one less emotional pressure and more time to spend reading, walking in the mountains, or otherwise enjoying herself.

It was 1996 when Maurice Reedus, Jr. was led to what has become his unlikely career as the Cleveland Sax Man. And like the waitress, it led to feeling comforted by the idea that each time he played he could go home with money in his pocket no matter how many bills had come. In fact, on the first day he played his horn on the street, it was because he had no other way to return home from a rehearsal with the band with which he was then playing his sax.

Maurice reached East 9th and Euclid Avenue and paused just outside a CVS store. The bus would be coming, but he realized his pockets were empty. He had left the rehearsal without money. His only alternative seemed to be to walk the several miles to his apartment when he saw a relative, Kelvin Taylor. Unfortunately Kelvin also lacked bus fare.

The straight ahead jazz man could dig improvisation after all:

It was Taylor's street sense and a personal history of selling handmade jewelry to passers-by that caused him to suggest that Maurice play his sax at the corner and see if anyone might toss some change in his case. Maurice had no intention of asking strangers for money and he thought that leaving his case open while he played was almost as degrading. As he later explained, "I was downtown and I had no bus fare, and this guy [Taylor] told me to take my horn out and start blowing. And I was a little embarrassed. A little bit. So I started blowing it and these people started dropping in money and I kept on blowing it."

As Maurice remembers the day, he recalls that he made approximately $20 in a half-hour's time. If he could somehow repeat such street concerts on a regular basis he would be making more money per day than he had ever earned from a regular gig with a band.

Intrigued by the possibilities, Maurice returned to East 9th and Euclid the following day and then the day after that.

Ninth Street is a major crosstown road with high rise office buildings all around. Thousands of Clevelanders daily drive the street, often using it as a shortcut to Superior, St. Clair, Chester, Carnegie, Prospect, and other busy areas that cross its path from Lake Erie south. That was why it came as no surprise that a television news crew spotted the Sax Man and made arrangements to run a short film clip of his playing. It was a time before You Tube, the corner, and not the medium, going "viral." Clevelanders who had seen the brief human interest feature on Reedus made it a point to walk by East 9th Street and Euclid Avenue to see and hear him, throwing a dollar or more into his case. Some also followed him to wherever in the downtown area he was playing on the sidewalk. Frequently they gave him money in appreciation, making clear it was a tip for the entertainment and not a response to some homeless man

Chapter 16

Maurice Reedus, Sr. in Trouble

While the Sax Man was still in school learning to play his instrument, exploring working with other musicians, his father was having serious problems on the road. He had begun working steadily in the Cleveland area, though always limited in the money he was offered. "I had to play four years at $10 a week at a place on E. 77th." He spoke of places that would not let a black musician play when they first opened, such as the Top Banana in the Cedar Shopping Center. Then he told how they opened to everyone—"all along 105th and Euclid. I got to play on Cedar Avenue and what was called Jew Town (now the Glenville neighborhood of Cleveland.) when the blacks came in to live in 1948, 1949, 1950..."

The elder Reedus talked of clubs that were beginning to dominate the local night life for a black musician—the Mercury, Tijuana, Society Club, the Chatterbox, the Shangri-La, the

Alhambra and the Esquire, the LaRue on the corner of East 107th Street...

. . .

The hip older man was more than the bebop perform-er of his earlier years:

During this time rhythm and blues was in demand and Reedus learned to play whatever music a club owner would pay him or a group to play. This was also a time—the 50s and 60s—when a number of major singers were touring and making records. Many of them used a different group of musicians on the road than they did in the recording studio, the elder Reedus hired to back up a number of major performers when they recorded in the city. His work eventually was heard behind Cannonball Adderly, Dion, and others. He also both recorded with Nancy Wilson and befriended her when she performed in Cleveland, giving her a ride to Columbus where she had her next gig. By then Maurice, Sr. was in one of several bands with which he worked over the years, and the band's agent was also in Co-lumbus. He left Nancy Wilson at her hotel, then continued driving to Omaha, Nebraska, where his agent had arranged for him to play.

. . .

It was at Omaha's Imperial Hotel that the music career was in-terrupted by a thief. The hotel was to be his short term "home" while the band played at various locations in the city. The room had been arranged but Reedus had almost no money for personal use, nor would he until after the performances.

As was his habit, Reedus left all his clothing and personal possessions in his car, then took his horns inside the hotel, leaving them in his room as soon as he registered. The process took no more than five minutes or so, after which he went back outside to get the rest of his belongings. To his horror, the car and all his clothing were gone. He could play, but the clothes he wore on the stage, the clothes he wore on the streets, and the clothes he wore in recording studios were lost forever. His car, the one personal asset he had with him, was also gone. He not only had lost everything, the band members with whom he had been playing were all looking to go in different directions professionally. Under the best of circumstances, he, like so many other working musicians, was still working hand to mouth. There were no spare uniforms, no alternative form of transportation, no savings account with money he could draw on. He was delighted that his horns had been with him and thus not stolen, but everything else in his life was gone.

. . .

Maurice, Sr. began to pick up the pieces of his world. He knew that he needed the highest paying work he could obtain while forming a new band, this time called The New Fools. "I worked on the garbage truck for 14 months. I worked Opportunity Industrialization Center (OIC) recruiting people to go to college. Then I got together [with other musicians] and formed The New Fools again playing music and performing comedy around Omaha.

185

"I knew a lot of people in Omaha from previous trips. When I first lost everything, I was able to stay with friends. They never found the car." He began playing music around the city, building back his reputation and his contacts in the music world. He also worked for Creighton University teaching classes in black history while performing at night. "And then I just played that for a while."

Maurice still considered the Columbus agent his band had used to be his representative. He also began performing with comedian Bill Cosby who was taking a break from playing basketball and doing stand-up. He had enjoyed a successful television show, *I Spy,* and was just having fun without special commitments. He originally met Maurice when both were playing clubs located around the Michigan State college campuses in Lansing, Michigan. Reedus performed there twice a year for two weeks at a time. It was chance that they met up in Omaha, Nebraska.

Cosby respected the older Reedus' talent as a comedian and suggested he audition with CBS Television in New York where two of its executives were looking for a male on-air salesperson to represent Florida orange juice in the New Jersey area. He would be partnered with singer Anita Bryant and the pay was such that he could stop hustling for jobs and enjoy success for a while.

Neither Reedus nor Cosby realized that the CBS advertising executives were sexually interested in Reedus. The moment he walked into their office he remembers their inappropriate behavior and their comments about Bryant.

Anita wanted to hog everything, the two men told Reedus. But they assured him that if they wanted to hire him, they could get around her then considerable influence with the network.

"They said they could get around her. They added that we can do anything we want to do... [pausing briefly for emphasis before winking at him and saying, "if you *cooperate*.

"I didn't believe that shit. You know what he was talking about? He was talking about someone hitting that Lincoln Tunnel [anal sex].

"I said I was doing this music thing and I thought I might get a comedy break. And they said, 'if you *cooperate*' I didn't know what I was supposed to do [sexually]. I didn't know if I was supposed to be the one who gives or the one who gets.

"Well, I said, I'll let you know I have to think about this."

One said, "Well, it's up to you, *Maury*..." I almost cried.

"I said, no, I couldn't do that." He decided that if accepting the sexual harassment was the only way to take his career to the next level, it wasn't worth it.

The younger Reedus and his path:

Pete Fulsom came into Maurice, Jr.'s life almost from the start of his professional career. He acted as a combination manager, promoter, surrogate father, educator, and as the musicians would learn, thief. Every story the musicians working with Fulsom had heard about promoters and the road seemed personified by the man. As Maurice explained:

"[I] met Fulsom only a couple of days before going on the road. He was the type of guy he'd pull up and if you wasn't ready, he'd pull off. We're going to use the bathroom and he'd pull off and be gone. We're out in the middle of nowhere and he'd pull off. He'd come back. Yeah. He was just real business, always wanted to be on time. We was never late with him. When we were on the road, he did all the driving. He liked driving. We was in a station wagon. Three people up front, three or four people in back.

"Fulsom weighed something like 400 pounds. John and Greg, the guitar player, would always sit up with him. Greg would be in the middle and John would be on the end by the window. And then me... me and Marvin would be in the back seat with the drummer, and then Terry and Charles would be in the far back seat. We had a U-Haul for the instruments."

. . .

"He'd make me so mad. He'd make me so mad, brother. I had to pee and he said, 'too bad. We ain't stopping nowhere. You got about four more hours to ride before we stop, so if you got to pee, you better pee in your pants. We got to be in town at a certain time. We got to be in town and we don't need no gas, so why are we stopping? He'd look at you. Sometimes he'd pull over to the side of the road and say, 'Get out!' And then he'd pull off, pull off with the car. And then he'd come back and get you. When it was time for us to leave he'd say to be in the parking lot at a certain time, and we'd come out there and he'd be gone. He'd be gone, man. Then he'd come back about 15 or 20 minutes later.

. . .

"We were in a station wagon, a 1969 station wagon. We had a manager, Fulsom, weighed three hundred something—400 pounds. We had three [rows of] seats, so it was like three in the front, four in the middle seats, and four in the back seats, pull-

188

ing a U-Haul. And Fulsom, Pete Fulsom, he was Lowell Fulsom the blues singer's brother. He was a big time blues singer. Our manager used to manage Johnny Taylor, big time blues singer. He was Johnny Taylor's manager for about five years before he (Fulsom) managed us [and booked the gigs.]

. . .

"We had to count the house. Every night there was an argument about pay. John Wilson arguing with Folsom about the money. Folsom would say, Motherfucker, there was no money. It's gone. I paid for the hotels. I gave you this. I gave you that."

"You mean people in the club and we ain't got no money? It's jam packed. All we get is $10 apiece. Hell, no.

"One time we got paid $7 apiece. I got paid $7... $7 and fifty cents. And Folsom be all the time talking shit." 'You ought to be glad you got that, motherfuckers.'

"That's the way he'd always be talking to us. He'd always be cussing us out.

" 'All you motherfuckers are stupid.' He told the backup, 'You no singing mother fuckers,' and he told John and the rest, 'you motherfuckers can't sing.' He used to be fussin' and fighting but he was our mentor.

"He used to have a briefcase filled with money. When it was time for us to get paid, he'd call everybody to the room and give us our little money." "We had motel money and we always ate. This was for 11 guys. He would take the money out the top, will this was for this and this was for that, and back then, everybody was going to the cleaners. We'd take the stuff to the cleaners, and he'd be paying the cleaner bill."

There were a lot of expenses for the 11 members traveling together, but Maurice felt he was taking some money for himself. Later John found a case of money hidden in the trunk of the car, and that led to Fulsom being fired.

. . .

Kelvin's Path:

When Kelvin Taylor got out of jail and opened his small custom jewelry shop to supplement the money he made selling on the streets, his best-selling items were brass name bracelets, brass initials, and name earrings. "We had a way we could take a half inch or three-quarter of an inch piece of brass, go get some stick on letters, drill between the letters, take the jewelry saw and cut the initials out, put a design on it, bend it, buff it up, maybe dip it in lacquer to preserve the shine. We charged five dollars a letter. Five dollars for the metal and five dollars for the letter. Me and my partner would take orders.

"What happened was Mr. Spears who used to have a wig and jewelry store in Shaker Square. I ran into him and he saw me with my jewelry case. He said, 'Let me see them earrings. You made them?' So I told him I had a little store. I made the earrings. And he told me he had a store at Shaker Square next door to Heinen's [supermarket] but down in the basement. He said, 'I'd like to order an initial set of earrings, a couple sample name bracelets, one of all of your fastest sellers.'

"I told him, okay, for me to really do that and to do that expeditiously, I'll have to send back to Chicago and get one of my understudies."

Calvin, Kelvin's understudy, was a man he had befriended when both were in Cook County Jail. What he did not expect was to meet again after their release. Each had boarded the El, the Chicago version of Cleveland's Rapid Transit System, at the same time and near the same stop. "I said, hold up, man, let me see if I can make a sale right quick." Kelvin had his sample case with him and saw a young woman he thought might be a customer. He walked over to the woman, threw open his earring case, and said, "Hold up, ma'am, would you like to look at my earrings?" She said, "Well, I'll take these, these, and these." I said, "Okay, Ma'am, well that will be $10 or whatever it cost back then."

The two men separated, but later that day Kelvin, known as Samad Samad among Black Muslims including his friend, received a telephone call. Calvin had been impressed with the way he made the quick sale and asked Kelvin to teach him the making and marketing of the jewelry. Taylor agreed, considering it payback for Calvin having looked out for him when they were both in the Cook County Jail.

"I started taking him around to the wholesale houses and showing him how to pick the jewelry. He got that down, and then I came on back to Cleveland where he sold jewelry.

"When I got out he would drop me a letter now and then. So he said, "Okay. We'll go get him a ticket."

"I got on the phone. I said, Hey, Calvin, I got this order but I need you. He said, "It's a good thing you called me because I just messed up $20,000 settlement they gave me for a cab hit me and I was just getting ready to stick up something. And I probably would have gotten killed or sent back to prison. Sure, I'll come. So he came and we went about the business of making jewelry and that's what we did for two or three years straight.

191

Calvin and Kelvin had two different styles of making jewelry, so Calvin set up his own shop, an indirect branch of the one Taylor ran. Then Kelvin ran into Brother Omar who had a head shop and black Afro-centric products in what was then the Black Muslim district around East 110th and Superior in Cleveland. Brother Omar was with the orthodox Muslim school. There were several in Cleveland, the families attending them believing that the methods for teaching both children and adults were the same ones the Prophet Muhammad used for teaching hundreds of years earlier.

"I used to make jewelry and Afro-centric pieces to Brother Omar and he sold them and he sold horns, too. I would go around to his shop   and we would talk jazz and what have you. And musicians would always come into his shop, so I said, "Well hey, man, I tried to play trumpet once. I can still read music. I got pretty good theory. And he said, 'Hey, you can use one of my horns.' So it was a saxophone and that's how I got onto the saxophone." This would be about 2000 or 2001.

"He said, I've got an old clarinet I'll sell you for $30. A clarinet and a saxophone have about the same keys except it can go lower and higher than the saxophone. The thing about the clarinet is you get trumpet, you get the particular nature of the clarinet and the saxophone. It can do all the jobs more or less. So I worked out with that and it got stolen. So I went back to Brother Omar, and he said, "I've got another old horn but it needs some work on it. And I said, okay, because I'm a little handyman/ fix-it man. But when he gave it to me [the needed repairs] it was way above my head. So I took it to Mister Brody, a repairman in Warrensville. He said, "Man, the person who sold you this horn is not your friend. If I did buy it, the most I would use it is for its parts because it's stuck beyond repair. He said, if I soak it in coal oil for a month, it still wouldn't work.

"I took the horn back to Brother Omar and he told me that if I couldn't have money I couldn't have the horn so he took the horn back. "About a week later I ran into a street brother who told me he had a horn he wanted to sell. It was a Wurlitzer and he charged Kelvin $25, and I played that horn and I kept working out and working out. I even took that horn to California when I went there in early 2000 around the time of the O.J. Simpson trial for murdering his wife.

. . .

"I lost my leg somewhere between '83 and '85 in Chicago in the Ida B. Wells Project. Chicago is well known for its gang warfare. Cabrini Green was first and Ida B. Wells was not far behind. And then you had Stateway Gardens... But anyway I was in the territory I really wasn't supposed to be. I was cutting through with my earrings and I had a few bags of weed on me, too. And the word got out that I was selling on their turf. Like I would cut through there going to the next street which was called like 35th and King Drive. I would cut over to 39th Street. The shortcut cuts four blocks off the trip, but in the process there I knew a couple customers. And a lot of times that was like my little watering hole. As I went up there, the word got out—"The earring man is back over here." They didn't bother me about the earrings. It was the weed. So they came for me, and I always had this little .25-automatic I used to keep. They had me cornered so I had to jump out of a four story window. And they was coming and there was no other way out, so I dived through the window. I came down.

"The Lord blessed me that I still had enough consciousness

to grab on to the third story level, and that took some of the momentum out of the fall. So then I couldn't hold on to the window and I fell the rest of the way. Fortunately it was dirt. Fortunately I didn't get hit by one of those windows that was swung open, the edge of that.

"God was with me all the way on that. When I got up, I fell back down, and I said, Allah, I can't walk. I can't walk. Oh, Allah, what's wrong? I can't walk.

"And then two teenagers—they couldn't have been more than fifteen or sixteen – they picked me up, one on each side. They said, "Are you a Muslim?" I said, yes, and by this time I could hear the siren of the ambulance. They drove up and scooped me up but I was still in a state of shock. I kept trying to sit up. "Why I can't walk, man?" And he kept pushing me down, trying to control me. "If you don't calm down, I'm going to have to restrain you." So however I got under control... Everything seemed to be just like a heat wave. You know how you see heat coming from a radiator.

. . .

One of the guys who found me in Chicago said, "I remember you. You know my sister." His sister was a girl who used to buy earrings from me. You see, I knew a whole bunch of people from the earrings, people they knew of me but I didn't know them. I was on my way off to the hospital after that.

"I wasn't playing [music] back then. I was selling my wholesale jewelry and other commodities. See, I didn't really get back to playing until I came back to Cleveland sometime between the 90s and the 2000s.

'Especially when I was in the joint, when I didn't have my mouthpiece to buzz on, I always dealt with my theory, when I start something, I stay on it. I could even when I was in the joint, but I couldn't access the horn. "I would say about 15 or 16, that's when I really got the music spirit. I had to have jazz. That's all it was to it.

"I really first became a Charlie Parker devotee when I got my first Omni book. That's a collection of all his music and that's been within the last at least ten years ago. But prior to that I had all musicians, I was proud that I was a Coltrane man. Trane was my guy and he still is. On the playing level. When I compare... if I take music and put it side by side, Charlie Parker's things that he write and with the things that Coltrane write, I got to go with Charlie Parker because the way he utilizes the staff, the lower, upper, and middle registers, it's just fascinating. I love to watch cartoons with the sound off and the jazz on."

The injury from leaping from the projects was as much an unexpected opportunity to focus on music as jail time had been. But first Kelvin established a jewelry business inside the hospital.

. . .

"The doctor said that my ankle was shattered so bad they couldn't put it back together. If they tried what they called 'heroic surgery,' he said that I would never walk right again, and probably in the end I would have it cut off anyway, probably, plus I would have all the marks on my body where they had to take veins and muscle tissue, so I said it was going to be one cut now or many cuts in the future so I prefer the one cut. I just

195

turned that negative thing into a positive thing.

"When they got me back up from the operation room they had a towel over it and the nurse came. When I saw that hole in my ankle, it was about like that coffee cup and yea deep. I knew that was bad.

"The doctor said they would have to take the leg."

Chapter Seventeen

Kelvin

"I was in the hospital for about 90 days. While I was there I made jewelry because they had me in traction. My one leg while they was trying to save it. So to keep myself busy I had my friend Calvin bring down my jewelry tools, my sheet metal snips, my jewelry saw, my Optivisor, a few patterns plus I clipped patterns out of magazines, things I thought would make good earring patterns. The hospital staff didn't say nothing so long as it's not creating a loud ruckus or nothing like that.

"What I would do, when I'd be sawing the jewelry, the jewelry dust that would fall, I kept a towel in my lap. It would fall in that.

"By me making jewelry, consequently, I got friendly with all the nurses. The nurses were coming from all over Michael Reese Hospital. "There's a guy over in Baumgarden there making jewelry, will you should see him. He's got one of those things on his head. He's just making jewelry."

"They started putting in orders—you know, 'Could you make me a pair of Ts, a pair of Ss, or whatever.' So then when I saw that, I told my friend Calvin, well bring me down some incense and oils. So he brought the incense and oils, so then my room turned into a great, massive fragrance house.

"All my roommates never stayed long. Or maybe that was because   I was there so long because they were trying to see to what extent the fractures were going to fall back in place.

"So after about 90 days when they saw that it wasn't [going to heal] that's when they moved into the next phase. So the most that roommate would stay would be about a week or so. So that made for conversation, like, man, how did you get into that? And it brought about other things. "I joined the Muslims in, I think, '61 here in Cleveland. You see my father was a barber on 39th and Scoville. The Texas Barbershop. And he would always read the Muslim paper, the *Muhammad Speaks*, and I was fascinated with the pictures, and by it being such an oddity at that time, and not only that, by me growing up in the projects at that time, some of the toughest gangsters, most notorious bad boys, all of them was turning Muslim. The next time I saw them, they had their shirt and ties on, and they knew the papers, and like... *whaaaatttt*? That struck me, too. I said, I got to see this, and that prompted me to start reading the paper. That stirred my curiosity.

"So then, the guy I used to sell when I was in the marijuana business... you see, I was just sixteen at the time... and we had a weed house at 137th and Kinsman up over the drugstore. His brother, "Deacon," Edward White, he joined the Muslims. And when I saw that, I thought, man, this is something going on here. So my friend who I was in the weed business with, he went one time and when he came back he said, "Kelvin, you got to go." So he was telling me bits and pieces about it, and then from what I was reading in the books and newspapers that my father had, one day I stole a car from down here in Cleveland and I said, "I'm going to put this car up and tonight at 8 P.m. I'm going over there to see what all this is about. So that's what I did. I went to the mosque on 118th and Superior." "I went there and I saw through the service, and I was fascinated. It was just so different from anything that I knew.

"I continued about my comings and goings and things. And by this time my father had bought the book *Message To The Black Man In America* and I was reading that. So right along to that period there that was when I decided I was going to make the trip up to Chicago to make that so- called fast money by getting this car that I stole. I went to Chicago, got stopped in Indiana,

"After that I took it around to a dark hole on Beaver Street— dark hole means that it was secluded—and I had had another car, too. Because the car that I stole, I took the tires off it because it had good rubber on it. I took the rubber off and I took the golf clubs out of the back and I put them in the other guy. It was a Buick if I remember—60 series—so I drove the tires and the golf clubs away and the guy gave me $200 for the whole kit and caboodle.

"Things like that, you know various people that buy things. Like I knew a guy that owned a garage. "I'll take the rubber. In fact, I'll take it all. So he gave me the money and then I went and bought my own reefer bags. I didn't have to be in business with nobody."

"The original contact... my friend, Dean, had that. But what it was, when I got my own contact, I bought from Dean. I was like a down line distributor and he gave me the regular whole-sale price with maybe an extra $50 or so for his pocket.

"The Indians got the hotels. The Ethiopians have the IHOPs, the hotels, and the 7-11s. So that's what I did with that particular car, there. "So after that I'm back to my regular comings and goings, selling weed, reading my books and my papers. Every chance I get I would go out to the mosque because it was fascinating. When I took the trip to New York and got into that trouble, that's when I joined. I wrote my letter to Chicago. You have to write your letter of acceptance. 'I desire to accept my own. I want to join the religion of Islam.' The letter was expected to be more work than a routine contact. Every letter has to be perfect. Closed, no open As, e's, things like that. All T's must be crossed, all I's must be dotted. It has to be a perfect letter. You mail that to Chicago and then they send you back what's called your "X" so I was in the penitentiary. While I was in the penitentiary I served as a lieutenant, as the minister, before I was released.

"Then, on getting out, when you come back to society. When I got off the bus I went straight to the temple. I didn't even go home first. And when you get there, then you have to write again.

"Elijah Muhammad, he had always told us that there was white Muslims. He said, but the reason I'm not propagating Islam to the Europeans in America, number 1, it's not a glove that would fit their hands in America.

"Secondly they know more about Islam than you do. They've always been exposed and had a knowledge to Islam. I'm teaching you all this because I'm trying to raise you up, and all my efforts and energy... this is all I can stand trying to deal with the so-called Negro as a people so don't be all bent out of shape and be concerned about them because the white people desire to join Islam. They know what to do. They've had Islam before you. Even the prophet Mohammad was a white man.

"Today I'm what you call a Universalist. I take all the good from all the religions. I try to be part of the orthodox Islam here in Cleveland but they turned it into a clique. It's a clique. So I just stopped going. I read my Koran. I say my prayers. I try to do my good and I play my music. That's me today."

. . .

Chapter Eighteen

Cousins

Kelvin Taylor (distantly related to Maurice by Mrs. Reedus' second marriage) was an odd contrast to the Sax Man when both were on the street, albeit at such different locations that passers-by usually heard and saw one or the other but not both. Their different skills were obvious from the ease of playing by the Sax Man and the effort of Taylor whose missed notes and inappropriately changing tempo sometimes made him seem like a music wrangler desperate to corral runaway notes into a recognizable song.

The disparate cousins developed separate fan bases, separate followers who made a point to stand and listen to them play each time they heard their distinctive horn work when going to or from home,　to or from an office, to or from a restaurant or sporting event. Taylor took pride in the continual development of his skills and delighted when a passer-by stopped to talk about the music, musicians, and the world of jazz. He, like The Sax Man, was occasionally paid to perform for a party, and also like the Sax Man, albeit with far less frequency, he would receive a surprising tip of as much as $100 or more.

The Sax Man was living primarily from the money dropped in his case. Taylor used the sax to supplement the small disability check he received each month prior to his death during the winter of 2012–2013.

The Sax Man has played before some of the largest audiences available to a touring musician. Taylor usually played for a handful of men, women, and children who happened to pass him by.

The Sax Man is a showman. The way he dresses, the way he moves while playing his instrument, all make clear that the streets are as comfortable for him as any stage on which he has performed. Taylor never worked with a professional band, never traveled from club to club, never had to "hook" an audience with his music. Yet each man appeared to have received enthusiastic support from Clevelanders who paused to hear them play.

Maurice Reedus, Jr. has also played for parties and special events. He performed in the rotunda of Cleveland City Hall while photographs taken by this author were on display. He played Christmas shows in the Galleria Shopping Mall. And he had a standing gig to play for a St. Patrick's Day Parade party given by a lawyer who likes the sound of the Sax Man's horn.

What makes Maurice special, far more than most street musicians in other cities, is his ability to be a magician of memories. His musical presence unlocks the childhood we often are embarrassed to admit we all carry in our hearts, intending to revisit before we die though rarely achieving that reality.

Play a few riffs and suddenly old men and, more frequently, old women have the gleam in their eyes reminiscent of the enthusiastic first day of high school band practice when the mastery of an instrument still seemed as though it would take only a week, maybe two, to be followed by Thanksgiving and Christmas concert performances in the school auditorium. They knew the feeling of their first reed, of clearing their first mouthpiece, of the resin bag and the shoes that sank into the playing field after a long, slow rain gave the earth the stability of quick sand.

"I got my first sax when I went to Kennedy," one person may say, remembering the date and store where the purchase was made. Another might mention Heights High, and a third might bring up Brush. They might have forgotten the boy or girl with whom they shared a first kiss or even the person with whom they went to the senior prom, but they will say, "I got my violin my second year at Shaw," or I played "French Horn at Adams." "Snare drum at Euclid." "Bells at Garfield." "Bassoon at Orange."

One afternoon, as the curtain is about to rise in the theater and the red coated ushers are hurrying the last lingering patrons to their seats, there is a moment just outside when Maurice is confronted by a fellow musician— perhaps 70 years old, perhaps 80 years old, and moving shakily to the beat of a band crisply marching on the playing field of memory. The old man is transported back in time to when music filled the stands jammed with cheering spectators, many of whom are remembered only through faded yearbooks and wall mounted images ever fewer classmates can recall. But just as the Sax Man returns again and again to that moment in 1975 when 80,000 people rose as one to cheer his solo, so some of the strangers who patronize the theaters of Playhouse Square return to their own special time and place, the Sax Man's solos the key to unlocking the memories of long ago sights, sounds, and happiness.

. . .

There are days when it seems that the Sax Man triggered a shared emotional healing experience by his presence. To the surprise of this observer, Kelvin Taylor had encountered some of the same reactions when he spent Saturday morning working at playing his horn near the West Side Market just down the street from the apartment in which he had been living. Kelvin had no illusions about the quality of his playing and the fact that the primary reason passers-by thought he was greatly improving was because he was such a poor player when he started.

Before his death Kelvin recognized he would never have the musicianship of the Sax Man but he satisfied himself with working to be a better musician with each passing day. He spent hours mastering one song, then moving on to the next, slowly building a repertoire he knew might never be completed but which brought him obvious pride in the effort.

"I guess it really is helping making people's day better or what have you. I guess they would just come over here on a whim... Just so many times, I'd just finish playing *Amazing Grace one* day, and this woman walked over to me and she said, 'You knew I needed that. You played that for me.' And I said, "Yes, ma'am, I sure did."

"Then some songs I played I said, 'Oh, man, I'm playing it but it might be a song I really need to hear. I'm playing it but I don't really feel it's in place. I'm getting all the notes per se on the paper and what have you. I don't feel satisfied with it myself and people come over and start putting money in and however, and man, I got to find this record somewhere cause I got to hear just the way the rhythm and the melody goes. And people come over and "Oh, man, that was nice." How could that be nice, man? I didn't feel that fun with it, you know, like I do with some tunes.

"It's just an amazing thing."

Chapter Nineteen

Maurice Reedus, Jr. Road Trip

Robert "Pete" Fulsom became the manager for Sly, Slick, & Wicked, the band for which Maurice was playing back-up on his first major tour. Fulsom, his 1972 Lincoln Continental Limousine transporting both the singers and musicians who comprised the traveling performers, was perfectly groomed in custom clothing that fit his 400+ lb. frame. He also understood that the musicians were early in their careers and limited in their experiences. He felt one of his jobs was to give them often obscene and always unwanted fatherly advice, frequently in front of the girls with whom they hoped to spend the night.

The Sax Man said, "We'd be talking with all the girls so he'd be coming over to the table and telling all the ladies, 'Don't be coming to the hotel if you ain't going to give them no pussy, ain't going to give them no money, ain't going to feed them, don't come here.'

"He'd be talking real loud at the table, 'Now don't be com-

ing to the motel unless you're going to give him something because if you're not going to bring him something, don't come
because we're on the road, traveling.' He would say all kind of
stuff.

"For a fat man he always smelled good. I mean, he never
smelled funky, brother. Never. Clothes and suits and never
smelled bad. Used to do all the driving."

. . .

John Wilson remembers:

"Fulsom wanted us to save money by letting women we met on
the road take care of us. These women, usually strangers to the
group, fantasized about being intimate with us. They would sit
at a table and decide which of us they would go after to spend
the night or a lifetime.

"Pete used to embarrass some of the younger musicians by
going up to the girls when he caught them talking with us and
tell them, 'If you ain't going to help them out, if you ain't going to feed them, give them some money, give them sex, don't
come in [to the hotel rooms—usually a Motel 6]. I'm telling
you that right now.'

"The Fulsom way meant that the girls or their mothers would
cook meals for us and often provide us a free place to sleep.

"Let's say it's the first time you come to the gig. There are
going to be some girls waiting backstage. I used to tell the
guys, the younger generation, I never had what they'd call a rap
where you sit down and you have to talk up on a girl. We didn't
never need that. The girls were always waiting. "This cut the

208

overhead, though it wasn't always comfortable. I remember spending one night sleeping on four kitchen chairs pushed together. Another place, one of our sax players, Maurice Reedus Jr., spent the night in a closet. Several girls shared the apartment and the one who liked Maurice lived in what was supposed to be a walk-in closet. She was short and he was tall, but you did the best you could.

"The keys to survival on the road always were the single women, along with the pimps and the gays. The pimp's the guy who watches the neighborhood. He's going to tell you which girls are married and which aren't. You would go to the town because the pimp is always going to go to the show and he's going to bring his ladies, so you'd make him feel special. You'd accommodate him—'Bring your top ladies, get your tickets, get your seats'—and that way you knew that he would take care of you. He'd say, 'Hey, man, don't mess with that girl. She's married,' or whatever, because he has a bead on everyone in the neighborhood.

"The gay guys who helped us were drag queens. They were flamboyant. I'd tell them, 'I don't go that way, but hey, man, where the girls is?'

"The guy would usually ask, 'Can you let me and my friend come in free?' "And we'd say, 'Absolutely.'

"So then he wants to help us. 'Well, see that girl there? Don't mess with her. But you like that girl there? I'll get her for you.' So they kind of kept an eye out for you and they'd look out for you.

"The problem was with the girls who were determined to get involved with one of the group even if they were married. They wouldn't wear a wedding ring, and they'd lie to you because you wouldn't know anything about them. Then you'd meet their husbands and that could be deadly."

· · ·

The Nova Scotia adventure:

"I'll never forget that gig," said John Wilson. "It (Halifax) was the hardest gig that basically we had to do because it was three shows, fourteen days straight and no days off.

"We didn't know what we were getting into because I had never heard of (Halifax) other than in history books. I knew nobody that ever came there. I didn't even know they had black people at all. The crowd (where they played) was fifty percent."

Fulsom had been fired, according to Wilson, and "we got the gig out of a booking agency out of New York."

Wilson:

"We drove [to Nova Scotia] in two station wagons that we were using at that time. There were eight of us plus we was pulling a trailer. When we got to Maine it had rained so much, we went by an old cemetery and the coffins were beginning to push up through the dirt."

The trip was four days, much of it on old roads with one lane in each direction and signs warning to look out for moose. The animal often weighed half a ton and hitting one would damage a car as much as a motor vehicle striking it.

"When we reached Nova Scotia and found the club, there was a band out of New Jersey just leaving called Fine Wine. And when we pulled up there, all the girls were hanging on the guys because they had been at their [Fine Wine's] gig. There was a drummer named Kenny Walker, and he came up to me I said,

'What do you do up here?" They watched the girls with the earlier band and were convinced they wouldn't have any fun.

"But here's the thing. As soon as the [Fine Wine] bus turned around, the girls who were crying stopped crying and looked at us. Just that quick."

The band members were startled but pleased. The girls were fickle, and it was fairly obvious that no matter what had happened before, Maurice and the rest of the band were going to score.

"So we went to the hotel and then started working the gig," said John.

Nova Scotia presented other problems, though these related to the business of performing. The leader of Fine Wine came over to Sly, Slick & Wicked to warn them about the crooked club owner. He was notorious for cutting promised pay. "If he booked you for a dollar," Wilson related to Maurice and the rest of the band, "He would try to pay you 75 cents."

As it turned out, the booking agency knew about the problem with the owner. When it came time for Wilson to collect the money they were owed, he was told to place a call to New York and have the manager get on the phone. Whatever the booking agent told him, all the money was paid. They were fortunate. Many of the clubs would succeed in "stiffing" the talent, and as each Reedus learned in turn, no matter how big an act a group might be, they were usually relegated to what was known as the Chittlin' Circuit. These were the mostly Black owned clubs where they were always welcome to perform.

Frequently the Chittlin' Circuit clubs were built for some other business—a bar, a restaurant, an auditorium. A stage might be built on the inside, the space so small that the audience was sitting almost nose-to-nose with the musicians. In several places around the country, the clubs either lacked electricity or they did not have enough to power the musicians' amps and other equipment. In those instances it was common for the club owner to go next door and stretch a long extension cord from the neighbor's wall outlet across the driveway and into the Chittlin' circuit club.

The name "Chittlin' Circuit was not so derogatory as it might seem given the nature of some of the clubs. There were major clubs featuring top entertainment and seating several hundred as well. But the name Chittlin' Circuit told the audience that blacks were welcome, something not always the case including in larger cities such as Cleveland, Ohio. There were also the black and tan clubs, a term meaning that audiences of all races were welcome.

While some of the clubs were built as night spots where local music fans could come to enjoy whichever individual or group was performing that week, others were converted warehouses, community centers, restaurants, and other buildings with large spaces in which to build stages. Some were beautiful. The rehab results with other clubs varied with the owner's finances and willingness to settle for the minimum work necessary to still draw a crowd. Some either had no electricity or too little to support the amplifiers, electric guitars, and other equipment the performers needed.

One makeshift club relied on the largesse of the owner of the house next door who allowed traveling performers to share the electricity. Weekend nights would see him bring out lengthy extension cords plugged into electrical outlets in whatever home or business was adjacent to the club. The food offered was limited in most of the clubs. The cheapest was always the pork rinds—Chittlins—covered with a hot sauce. One step up would be places that had a grill so they could offer fish, chicken, or hamburgers. Drinks varied, though it was rare for the clubs to have a liquor license. Instead, some sold the small liquor bottles offered on many airlines. Others had moonshine whose safety was always suspect. And a few of the clubs offered "set-ups." For what was $2 when Maurice was first on the road, a customer would be given a pitcher of ice and four Cokes. The customers could drink the soft drink or they could bring a bottle of the hard liquor of their choice.

The Halifax, Nova Scotia club might have been considered a black-and- tan joint from the Chittlin' Circuit, but there was no local competition. "It was the only joint in town," said Wilson. "...a full blown club that held about 700 to 800 people."

As to the experience, "The first thing that happened was that the club girls would come up and give the people flowers. But this one girl had her sights on one of the members of the band. She was a very attractive girl. About the second or third night she kept coming in wearing the same thing every night. It was a red dress, a red-like velvet dress. She also did the same thing. She'd come up to the stage and hand him a rose."

The girl quickly became an overnight visitor, spending her nights with the band member in a room not too far from the stage. It was close enough so that one night they heard him exclaim, "Oh, man...!"

"He came running down to my room shouting 'John, open up. John, open up.'"

The band member had John look at his private parts that were covered with a rash. The girl had obviously been too friendly for too long with too many different members of too many different bands.

Some of the band took the musician to the hospital for treatment of whatever sexually transmitted disease he had.

Arrangements were also made by the hospital to pick up the girl and treat her as well. Both recovered from the experience.

Maurice learned about what had happened and had already heard that the doctors said both the band member and the girl would fully recover. The news had not calmed the musician with the rash so Reedus strolled over to him and sadly said, "Oh, man, you're going to die."

Soon Maurice started seeing a different girl, also a fan and either not promiscuous or much luckier than the other one. She had a place of her own they found more comfortable than the hotel the others were staying in during the gig. Before each show he would go from the girl's house to the hotel and then all piled into the cars and went to the gig.

John Wilson decided one day to go over to where Maurice was staying. "And I went over to the place and there was another girl living there. It was real small and I said, 'Is Maurice here?"

The girl, apparently the roommate of the one Maurice was seeing, said he was. But Maurice was well over six feet and the house seemed almost too small for him alone.

"Where is he?"

The roommate pointed to a door that obviously led to a closet. There were two sliding doors covering what looked like an opening of maybe eight feet wide. One door slid one way when you opened it and the other door slid the other way.

She encouraged Wilson to knock, and when he did, the door slowly slid open. "There was Maurice in the closet. She had a bed there and a mattress, a twin mattress, and it was just deep enough for the twin but someone Maurice's height could stretch out very easily. "That's where she was living. I knocked on the closet door and she opened it up. Maurice looked up from where he was laying on the bed and said, 'What's up, Pete?' That's where they were living together when he was there."

. . .

"It [Halifax] was a real hard gig," Wilson continued. "It was three shows a night from 9 o'clock in the evening to 3:30 at night. We were working six hours."

The pressure of so intense a schedule would have been exhausting under any circumstances, but in the little town where they were performing there was no other activity... no other night clubs or live entertainment. They had to fill the time with a show that would keep the customers lingering and happy.

Wilson explained, "So we wouldn't be totally wiped out, the band would do the first set. We (Sly, Slick, & Wicked) would do the second set. And this is when Maurice started doing his comedy act in order to keep the time rolling. We'd have the band play, then Sly, Slick, & Wicked, then the band again, and then Maurice. The sets were a long and hard gig seven days a week."

"During that time, one of the members of the band asked another member if he could use his shower. I don't know what was wrong with his, but he was told, yeah. "The room was right across from mine and   I couldn't sleep well at night. So what I did was I opened my door, and when I opened my door, there was water coming out of the room where the band member had gone to take a shower, there was water coming out of the room.

"I went running back in my room and used the phone to call his room. There wasn't any answer so I went back out and began pounding on his door."

The musician, a heavy sleeper, did not realize anything was wrong when he bolted awake, startled by the knocking. Wilson heard him get up, then shout, "Oh, man...!" as he slipped and fell on a pool of water.

The musician who had borrowed the shower was fully clothed and oblivious to the damage he was causing. What he had never told the other band members was that he was a Vietnam vet who suffered from a form of Post-Traumatic Stress Disorder, apparently triggered in part by the exhaustion from the intensity of the road trip. He didn't seem to be having a flashback and he never explained what he was thinking or seeing in his mind. He just stood washing himself, his shirt off, his pants and shoes on, and a hat on his head. "Was I messing up?" he asked innocently as he looked at his friends as they reached in and turned off the water.

The musicians knew they had to get the troubled vet back to the states as soon as they finished the gig, but there was one more experience. It was late morning when Wilson heard laughter coming from down the hall. He went out, and there was Maurice laughing so hard that he had slipped down the wall and was holding his sides, convulsing. All he could do was point to the room where the troubled band member was staying. The door was open and once again the musician was having a reaction to past trauma. This time, though, he was standing before a mirror, the only clothing being his hat, holding himself as though in the midst of a sword fight."

The woman who focused on getting to know Maurice during the two weeks was a nurse who apparently was more serious than many of the others. She either fell in love with the Sax

Man or she came to want a commitment. The nature of the work and the town meant that they were in constant close proximity whenever he wasn't on the stage, and the nurse soon developed a plan for the rest of their lives. A competent nurse who had met all local licensing requirements could get a job in any hospital with an opening, and the work was just stressful enough that there were always openings. She knew that if she moved to Cleveland it would not take long for her to be employed by one or another of the region's many hospitals.

As the days passed, Maurice listened to the woman who soon was engaged to marry him talk about where they would live in Cleveland, how they would live with his periodically being on the road, and the family of which she would soon be a part. Eventually the talk got around to planning the wedding itself.

Maurice managed to convince his supposedly soon-to-be bride that she and he should spend every spare moment together. Only when the band was pulling out of town should she call his mother and together they would plan the wedding for when he returned to Cleveland and she was able to join him. It sounded romantic. However, the Sax Man knew his mother would be the one to have to tell the nurse that he was already married. Both women would be mad at him but he would only have to face the wrath of one.

Chapter Twenty

The Emotional Disconnect
of the Sax Man in Love

["Music is what feelings sound like."—author unknown]

One of the more difficult areas to understand is the emotional disconnect of the Sax Man in love. The story of the engagement to the Halifax based nurse seems to be that of a callous youth with the perpetual sexual arousal of an adolescent and the sensitivity to others of a similar nature. But that seems too simple when trying to understand.

There was a woman in Kentucky who loved Maurice without illusions. She knew his eccentricities. She knew that he periodically used street stimulants. She was caring for her grandchildren, and though she spent many a night with him when someone else was caring for the little ones on a weekend or during a vacation from school, she made clear that a full commitment would not happen until she could trust him to be more responsible towards himself and others.

The Sax Man made periodic trips to Kentucky to see the woman they both considered his fiancé. He would play before sporting events and at a mall, always doing well. He was also comfortable with her talking about both his good points and his less than honorable actions including occasionally having a past involving "sticky fingers."

The Kentucky romance was the most serious one I experienced with the Sax Man, the most serious since the time he once spent with Chevonne. As Luwana, the woman who, for many years, would be the most important in his life, at least until he let loneliness and the opportunity for casual intimacy with others destroyed the relationship. As she explained:

It was June the 12th of 1998. Maurice was in a band playing at a club called A-1-A. I had went out with a friend. We were going out for a drink. We went upstairs because they had one band downstairs, one band upstairs, and another section with a DJ. They [Maurice's band, one with which he played when they went on the road and needed a sax player.] was playing on a patio upstairs and you could sit down and watch the volley ball game.

Luwana: *I was sitting back and enjoying the game, and there was this guy who was in a Karate outfit. And I just kept watching his choreography and I was saying, "He's cute! He's cute!" And so my girlfriend was like, "Say something to him. Say something to him."*

And I said, "No. No."

I got to meet the [band] manager and her husband. They said they were on their way to Florida, but on their way back through they would be stopping in Kentucky. So I got to meet all the band members but I wasn't saying nothing to Maurice, though. He was outside doing push-ups, and I was like, "Look at him!" I thought it was strange, but it was unique, too.

My girlfriend and I kind of got into a bet when we knew they were coming back. It was going to be my fortieth birthday, and so I said I'm going to do something I've never done in life before." She was going to talk with Maurice. "And she said, 'Well, I dare you because I had never in my life approached a man on my own.'

And she said, 'I'll bet you a dinner that you won't say nothing.'

They came back and it was my birthday, June the 20th, we got there and I just kept watching him. I said there's something about his eyes. I said, 'oh, he's got the prettiest eyes. And he's fine! He's fine!'

They took a break and the friend bought a CD. Maurice was outside doing sit-ups, his army sit-ups. And I had counted 25 and I was like, 'okay.' So when he came back inside, I walked up to him and said, "Excuse me. I usually don't do this. This is out of the ordinary but I still got to say something. You are fine! And he kind of just smiled, and I said, I'm not trying to be funny or nothing, but you are a fine man." And I proceeded to walk away and I just watched him the rest of the night.

So after the night was over, he said where they were staying at the hotel and asked if we wanted to come over to the hotel, and I was kind of skittish about it, but my girlfriend had met one of the other guys so she wanted to go. So we got to the hotel and it was like three of them staying in a room together. It was Maurice, the band leader, and Ghani. So my girlfriend was talking to the band leader and I just kept sitting there looking at him and he was just moving around, doing a whole lot of things. We really didn't have much conversation because I was shy and he was shy, and so they was going to pull out the next day, and so when I got home, I called him. And that's when we talked on the phone. He gave me his home number, his mother's address, his address. He said would you mind coming back out here tomorrow before we leave? So I went back the next day, my girlfriend and I, and we got there just as they were packing up. And I noticed Maurice was doing everything.

He was putting the bags in the car. He had one of those carts that

you pull with the clothes on. And I was like, why isn't anyone else do-
ing anything? And it was like, 'Maurice! Maurice! Do this. Do that.
It was an attitude. And I was like, why are you doing everything?
Why are they not doing anything? It's not fair.

And my girlfriend said, 'you act like he's your man
already.' And I was like, 'He's going to be.'

So he told me when he got home he would call me, and he did. He in-
vited us up, so we came up the Fourth of July, and he lived in South-
gate Towers. And so we came up and we stayed for four days, and
he proceeded to take us around Cleveland, and he showed us where
Gerald Levert lived, where he grew up, all types of different stuff, so
we kind of got to know each other.

From that point on we could have conversations. I proceeded to come
to Cleveland more.

I had to meet his mother and I was really scared. He said, "She's down-
stairs." And I'm like, I'm not going down there like this and meet your
mother for the first time."

He said, "Come on. She'll be all right." I'm scared. She's going to
come up. So I went downstairs and she says, 'You shouldn't be scared
to meet me. All I can say is for you. I really feel sorry for you."

And I was scared to ask what that meant.

She wanted to go to the store with her son's new relationship and Maurice's sister. *I didn't want to go the way I was dressed.*
She said, 'You scared to meet me because you got on biker shorts?'" I
was small. I just wore everything skin tight. I still was scared. And
I wanted to ask her what she meant about that [feeling sorry for
me]. So she brought me back to the apartment.

So around the end of August I came back up by myself and planned
to stay a week. And he told me he was on probation, and I asked him
why he was on probation and he didn't tell me the truth. This guy had
stolen something and they got him for receiving stolen property. He left

221

to go see the probation officer and he didn't come back. And then I got this phone call and he said, Baby, I got locked up.

I said FOR WHAT?

And he said, for dirty urine.

And I said, how long are you going to be detained? And he said, 'I don't know.' And he said I'm getting my probation officer lady's name. Call and talk to her.

And she's like, 'I don't know. He's probably going to do some time.' And I said, 'how much time?' And she's like, I really can't elaborate, but he told me that he would call.

I started crying because at that point I didn't have any money. No money. No money. No nothing. Just my car and a full tank of gas, and I really didn't want to leave because I had just started liking him.

I called home, crying to my daughters. Maurice has been locked up. I don't have money. I don't have nothing to eat. I want to see what's going on. My sister caught the Greyhound to come up here with me.

I said, I'm not going nowhere. I said I want to see what's going on. So we did. Went to court, and that's when everything started coming out. Stuff was coming out. And I found out that he had been fighting this for like ten years. And he had a judge who was really nice because he talked with me off the books. He really liked Maurice. He knew Maurice wasn't a bad person, but this had started about ten years earlier, and what had happened was Maurice had been with somebody who had been stealing, so his lawyer told him to say that he had a drug problem. So that's how it got started with him on probation and he had to do urinalysis. He had a couple of them over the years.

So I thought, okay, everybody deserves one mistake. I found out your one mistake. If anything else ever happens again... I don't do this. It's not my cup of tea. So then I decided I wanted to be up here.

I wanted to stay up here for him. And he had to go to Rehab, and his mother kept saying she wasn't going to pay the rent on the apartment. She's been going through this too long.

"Well, I can't afford it and take care of home too 'cause my last daughter was getting ready to graduate, and I already said I was going to leave Lexington when my last child graduated. Well the best things I can do is pay the utility bills and the telephone bill. And I said I'm going to get a job up here to get money to send home.

Then, when I found out he was going to have to do three years, I said, I'm not going to stay up here by myself. I'll put his things in storage and I'll pay the storage for him.

I got me a job and I stayed up here and I went to visit him three days a week. He was in the county jail but he wasn't there long. They moved him to a rehab that was off E. 55th. It was a house on Cedar.

So I would go three times a week and his counselor would tell me, 'Maurice is not taking this seriously.'

His mother, she had a tour bus company. I had talked with her about working part time, and she said they were in the process of selling it out. She was getting out of business.

Then he got out of rehab and he came home. I got him a job with me. We was processing inserts. Bookmarks. Then my car broke down and he was still doing the games. I would come down with him every day and stay with him. I thought it was unique. He said his back was hurting. Took him to the doctor and he was off for about a week so they let him go. I was going home at least every other weekend. Two weeks in I got another phone call. He got another dirty (urine). And that was like, okay. I really wasn't understanding so I learned from the rehab that I needed Al-Anon. It allowed me to understand what was going on. It allowed me to keep hanging in there. So I stayed and hung with him and everything, but I had went

223

home.

He had called to tell me that he wasn't going to be sent to prison; that he was going to get out. I told him, "I know what I heard the judge say. Yes, you are."

"No, babe, for real. For real. Because they don't have no room. They had sent him back to the county jail because he had gotten dirty in the rehab. They sent him home. He got released the very next day. They said he really wasn't supposed to go. He wanted to get a bus ticket to Kentucky but they weren't going to pay for it so they just gave him a ticket back to here. So he caught a bus ticket down to me. "I said, you know you're going to have to go to [AA] meetings. I had to put my foot down. You know, this is the only way I'm going to do it. If you're going to be a part of my life, I want you to have a positive feedback for them [her grandchildren] so they can see their granny's not with somebody who's doing something she doesn't approve of. He agreed and he did and he proceeded to get good jobs. He worked for the UK Hospital. He was there for about three months. Then he re-lapsed again and got into the VA program.

I never saw it—buying drugs. My daughters came to me and said they saw him buying it one night.

I was like, 'Saw who buy what?"

And they was like, Mom, we wouldn't lie to you.

We all lived in the housing project. They had their apartment and I had mine. When I came back home I decided I was going to sell the house, and then my ex-husband separated and said we're go-ing to sell it and split the difference. And I said I don't want to pay any more big bills. I just want to take my money and travel the rest of my life. I'm not giving to nobody else. And I was beginning to find that I had health problems. I started thinking about the fu-ture and I said I want to be somewhere I can take care of me and not depend on somebody else.

And so they (daughters) told me they had saw him cut between the buildings to cop some. So I waited on him and I said [to Maurice] did you buy something? And he's like no, no, no, no.

I said, "Don't lie to me." So I brought the daughter in his face, and she said, "Yes, you did, Mr. Maurice. Matter of fact, you bought it from my cousin.

He's like, 'no, no, no. I don't know why people's lying on me.

I forgave that because I didn't see it for myself. Then you have to do something. You have to do the drug testing and bring me proof. So he got in the VA Program and they got him a job in VA. Six months he did fine. Then he continued. And they (daughters) kept coming to see me and saying, 'Mom, we know you don't want to believe it. And I felt like my girls were looking at me like, 'What are you doing at forty years old? This is not you. You don't even like people who drink. They said, you must really love him.

I said I do, and so I said to him, 'You got to go back to Cleveland.' I'm not going to put you out, but he was calling his mother and saying negative stuff. We didn't want to be bothered with him. And she knew better. I was mad at her because she should have forewarned me what I was getting into. And that's what she meant about when she said, "I prayed for you." And she said, I'm just blessed that he has you." And that really put the tight rings on it. I was already in love with the man.

He didn't want to leave. So my middle daughter, April, she's the humble one. She's more like him. She said, you can come stay with me and just give Mama some time.

And I said, well, that's where you need to be. So he went and stayed with her when she only lived a few buildings away from me. And I'll still go up and see him and he'll come back and he'll tell me he's doing this and whatever.

One day a guy came to the house looking for him, and I got bellig-

erent. You put my daughter in danger. You put my grandkids in danger. I'm going to pay for your bus ticket. You're going to Cleveland today. He had called his mother and she had purchased the ticket. He hadn't told me. So he came back to Cleveland. We still communicate because I couldn't just let go of him. He's going to get it. He's just so sweet. A likeable person got a heart of gold. So he came back to Cleveland and I start commuting back and forth to Cleveland to see him. He got an apartment and I kind of put the utilities in my name, and I just kind of came to the point where I said, "Now look, Maurice, I'm going to tell you this. I'm not going to ask you any more if you're getting high. I don't even want to know if you're getting high so volunteer me no lies. So you're going to do what you're going to do, but I'm always going to give you warning when I come. Would you please give me enough respect to not do it for a week prior to my coming?

They were going to go to Florida. I had been on a number of gigs with them. Pat was real belligerent. She didn't like the women of the guys traveling with them because she thought they would be distracting them. Really what it was was she didn't like me because I was too headstrong and I could see he could make more money by himself. They were taking from him. They're charging you all for things you shouldn't pay for, like they had a gig in Akron. The mike messed up. Something else went out. And when it was time for them getting paid that night, they had to pay for gas and to pay for them to have to go to a music store to rent equipment. That's not supposed to come out of you all's pay. You all supposed to have a pool for that. So when they got paid, they got $25 for the night. So I begin to start speaking on this."

To the Sax Man's surprise and delight, Luwana, his new girlfriend had an understanding of both business in general and the way nightclubs, restaurants, and other spots offering entertainment could properly work with the acts that performed in their establishments. She looked at the receipts, including the money being paid, the legitimate expenses, the expenses inappropriately being charged against what the performers were earning, and other factors. She agreed to drive some of the musicians to their gigs and gained greater insight both from their talk on the trip and what she saw when they reached the clubs where they were playing.

Ultimately she felt that the musicians were not always receiving what should have been their fair share of the money paid by their fans to see them. She also learned that the manager would periodically try to get Maurice's mother to underwrite some of the gigs. And when she first met this writer, she asked for $1,500 to make a demonstration record to help promote the group.

The more Maurice's girlfriend learned, the more troubled she became. She was that rare individual who brought far more to the relationship than she received, and she did not mind the discrepancy. She wanted Maurice to succeed and if bringing her education and expertise to bear in their relationship, often alienating him from people he thought were friends but actually had been cheating him, she did not care. She wanted Maurice to be successful, whether that meant as a nightclub headliner or a busker on the streets of Cleveland.

The Sax Man was being cheated out of pay through his reliance on others. His new girlfriend also found that he was cheating himself. Without intending to do so, she became his organizer/manager for his work on the streets, and the overseer of the money earned by the bands with which he occasionally played.

"I started making mental notes. I said, Maurice you have so

many people who walk up to you. Your clients. And tell you they want you to play for them. You're not coordinated. So I'm going to take you beyond what you're not doing. We're going to start organizing. I'm going to be your business manager.

"For real, babe?" both Maurice and his new lover remember the shocked Sax Man saying.

She said, "I'm going to make you start following through on some of this stuff. I'm on the street here with you and people walking up and saying, 'Would you play for my anniversary? I'll pay you $75 for 30 minutes for my wife.' I said you're going to start following through with some of this stuff.

"Maurice is scared of disappointment," she told me. "If he can't make someone like him and he can go full-force with, and if I make a mistake then people are going to look down on him, cause even to this day, I've been with him... it will be ten years on the twentieth... If I tell him something, he says, "You always putting me down."

Then I have to tell him, "I'm not putting you down. I love you. I am trying to help you. So I've learned when you say something to him, he feels you're putting him down. You're talking bad about him. And it's not that way.

"I tried to get him going to school. I even took him where he was going over on Warrensville. When I was up here I could do the leg work, but as soon as I went home, it was excuses.

"[I also discovered that his mother has to control every dime he gets. She called me to ask what he made after the sporting event to see how much he's made."

The reality of Mrs. Reedus' involvement with her son's work, dating, and most other aspects of his life was mentioned frequently. Even Maurice, Jr. tended to joke about it, such as when he delighted in showing her the article I had written about him.

It was only after her death that he began carrying her photo-graph seemingly everywhere, though when discussing his parents, the person inevitably mentioned was his father.

Maurice's new girlfriend would not be intimidated. She was a mother, a grandmother, a single parent, and a woman of honesty, intelligence, and moral outrage when she felt that someone she cared about was being mistreated. She said that she told Maurice, "I'm not dating you *and* your mom... You are enough. Your mother's too much." She insisted that the Sax Man act like the adult his age showed him to be. She saw no reason why, each time he did a gig, that he had to account to his mother for how much he earned or how he spent the money.

"He has a disability, that's true. But I also know that if you hinder someone, they're not going to grow. His sister has never stepped outside the nest. Maurice so wanted to be like his father, which is a good thing. If he didn't, he would be home to this day.

"His sister and I have been out in the club together. I know what she can do. And I love her mother dearly, but I told her, 'You will not have a life until your mother dies.'

"It's a blessing that Maurice wants to be like his father because it has allowed him to get out in the world and not be controlled. But she still has X-amount of control over it and he's scared to let that go because he knows he's not going to do right. He knows he can call his mother. He can't call his father and say, 'Dad, can you pay my rent. I'm going to be put out.' You know you're grown now and that's okay. But she has a fight with the father within herself because he loves and respects his dad more than he does her, which I know he don't.

"His dream is to make a record with his Dad."

"And that's another thing. He had that chance to play with that band (Robert Lockwood, Jr. All Stars). His father told him, 'Son, I love you.' Sit right there in the club and told him in my face, 'but you're inconsistent.' And that's when he brought in two of his friends, and that was devastating. One of them still plays with them (All Stars) to this day, and any time he goes to that club (Fat Fish Blue where Lockwood and the All Stars performed weekly). And then they asked him to play.

They went down south a couple of years ago and they asked him to fill in. Oh, that was a dream for him to travel with his daddy. And then he came back and I know I was going to hear all the whatevers. They couldn't get him up. He kept disappearing. These are the things that are hurting you.

"He's scared to try to read. It's just a challenge. I say, what's it going to take?

"When I'm at home I say everybody in Cleveland's like, what's wrong with you? Because they feel he makes more contact with me... We just haven't heard from Maurice. We've just learned to accept it.

"The only time I get worried is when I see his mother's number [on caller ID]. I'm afraid she's going to call and tell me she found him dead or something happened to him. But I don't know what else I can do for you. "He was supposed to reunite with Sly, Slick & Wicked. Can't reach Maurice by phone. Gave people Luwana's number. I got people still calling me at home." [This was before the documentary was being made and a reunion concert was performed as representing in the documentary crew's mind the high point of his work and his life.]

It was with the woman who both loved him and accepted the reality of the poor decisions that frequently dominated his actions that he began to learn how to be independent of others, how to pay his own way in life. She helped him get a job to supplement the Sax Man's earnings on the street. She showed him how to go to the grocery store and shop for a week. She stayed by his side, explaining how to be responsible. And when he received an angry telephone call from his mother who could not reach him until March 17, he realized that he needed to include his telephone bill in with the basic necessities for which he had to pay.

Another harsh lesson related to the Sax Man's relatively frequent requests by regular passers-by to have him play for private parties. These were mostly casual corporate affairs—law offices, accounting firms, and the like—where he would be paid to come in and play requests as well as whatever other music he chose. One regular gig was St. Patrick's Day when a party was held on the ground floor of the office building in which the law firm was located. There was a catered lunch set-up near a massive window through which the employees, their families and guests could watch the annual Cleveland St. Patrick's Day Parade.

The pay per hour was more than he was averaging on the streets—a low of $40 on a typical night on up to $100 or more outside a sporting event—so he was assured of coming out ahead by working one night off the streets. And most of the events had a tip jar available for anyone who wanted to give extra.

The problem was that often the Sax Man would forget the time, the date, and the obligation. No one had ever trained him to keep a calendar of events and obligations. No one had ever explained basic business expectations even if his career was far from traditional. Once again his fiancée involved herself, having Maurice bring her the business cards and notes with dates and telephone numbers he collected.

The problem that arose was that Maurice was becoming too comfortable with his life and with Luwana who was debating how much more serious the relationship could become. But first she had to know what she was facing. "I needed to know how much he was spending on drugs. He had gone through detox. He had the nightmares, the lunging, the motor mouth when high. He had been run out o the low rent hotel where he had been staying."

Maurice focused on the clothing he was wearing when performing, as though so long as he looked nice, no one would know he was on drugs. "You can dress all you want. People who don't know you personally, who just know you as Cleveland Sax Man, they can tell you on drugs. They can see it in your face. They can tell when your pupils are dilated. You're fooling only yourself."

Then she added, "He wants to get his teeth fixed. They'll put him to sleep. Rehab got medical he was afraid otherwise. Pay for teeth. The problem is getting him up to be motivated.

"I have not been nowhere with him where he has not got a standing ovation where he played. It gives chills to you.

"His best is solo. Give him the center of attention, he blows you away. But if he's with a band, he's not really in tune to what's going on until it's his turn.

"I know he's dying. I know he's dying. He'll say, 'Whoo, girl, I just got in. Shoot, I know these pants are getting tight on me, because he knows that's what I want to hear, cause I told him, until you start gaining weight, until your face starts coming… When I met you you were a [pants size] 34/35 to a 36. You can wear a 28 now. I really can't stand to look at you. It's killing me, watching you die. And it hurts.

"When he comes in at night, taking his clothes off, and I'm crying on the inside, and praying, "God, please help him. I don't want him to die. I don't want to be a part of it. I don't want to sit here and see it.

"I love him much more away from me than I do face to face because it's killing me."

And always there was the omnipresence of Maurice's mother. "She wants me to commit to take care of him. She said, 'I was hoping that you're marry him.'

"I said I'm not going to get married ever, ever, ever again because I don't want to go through that. I said I wouldn't even make a commitment to you.

"Then she told me she took out an insurance policy on each of her kids and she wanted to put one on me. But I told her you're not locking me in like that because I don't know what the future will bring. I might die before him if I keep dealing with him. And she start laughing.

"She said because you're the only real female that he has dated. He really hasn't dated. They've been users. She said, I know that you care about him. I thought that after the first year because you were the only fool [who visited him in drug] Rehab.

"Everybody needs to be loved. I didn't fall in love with him because he's a musician. I fell in love with him because of the person he was.

She looked at Maurice and said, "If I had to deal with you every single day, we'd have been through a long time ago. Either you would do it my way or no way. My way would be that you would be in rehab and I would be going to see you just to make sure you go. But I've learned over the years that that doesn't work. If you don't want it, it's not going to happen. So that's how I've learned to separate myself. You can come to me and say I want to come down to Kentucky and I'm going to say you can come down here. You know my door's always going to be open. You can always come here.

"I feel safer here (Cleveland) about him than I do in Kentucky because I don't have to worry about nobody hurting him. You don't know these people down here. They could kill you. This is your surroundings.

"I said [to Maurice] the only reason you don't steal and you don't rob is because you can pick up that horn and go make $20 to get what you want. But he's had his little sticky fingers and I don't understand that.

"He was looking for approval from his father because, I guess, he was a junior and his father played the horn. But once he got that horn and had the ability to teach hisself, it was no longer to be my father. This is my dream. This is my music.

"I've listened to the stories from the seventies up to the present. All the people he's played behind. And if you don't enjoy something, you don't memorize that. If you get him on a good day, he can give you right down to the detail, the time, the date, the day of the week and all. He's told so many stories that on a good day I can repeat them for you. Sometimes I cut him off and finish his sentence for him.

"And I think that his second love is comedy. He'd really love to do stand-up comic.

"He's been in competition with his family and his father because everyone in his family is doing something that he thinks that is big. They work every day. There have never been any problems. Everybody is either a teacher, a principal, a musician. I'm just me. So I think he's always been in competition because he sat down and talked with me and said, "If I had big money, everybody would want to be my friend. Everybody would be Maurice. Everybody wouldn't be talking down."

"You should be in a position where you ain't always got to go downtown when a club closes. You get angry because you can't spend time with me on weekends because you always got to go make money because you're behind. That's you.

"I would love to come up here and hear, 'Well, Babe, I'm playing in such and such club tonight.' I don't want to hear well, I gotta go to the bottom to go make this money, and you leaving out at midnight and getting back at two to get the money to keep the rent people off your back. It's just not worth the headache. I'd just rather talk to you on the phone and see you periodically. And you know you can call me. I'm here. If something happens to you I'm there. And I know if I need him, I can call.

[There was a time] when everything was going wrong. I needed him. It took him a week to get the money for the bus but he came and stayed two weeks. I really appreciate it, but it's time for you to go home now.]

"I'm a reactor. If I care about you, I react. Like he came home one time from playing at the game and he said, Babe, you know that girl down there that sweeps the broom (Downtown Cleveland Alliance), she going to tell me I'd better not come around that corner. And he was literally scared to go back around that corner. I came down there with him and I want you to walk in front of me. And I think my sister had came up for a visit, and she's not a trouble maker either. She's low key. I say you walk in front of me. I dare her to say something today. And he say, Babe, don't say nothing. I do.

"He didn't want to go around that corner. He wanted to go

235

all the way around. "Now you go down there like you done all these years. And she was out there sweeping, asking people for money. You can just see him shaking in his boots. She didn't say nothing. I don't know what it was. I prayed for her to say something.

"So one day we came up here and my middle daughter, she's a reactor, too… She's just ready to fight. Soon as we got there he went to April to go to the woman. My daughter's here now.

"I was scared when I first told him, three years into the relationship, I said, 'Maurice, you're good but you could be better.' And he said, 'you're the first person to come and been scared to tell me outside of my father.' You know, you need to go to an academy. I went back to school when I was 38."

"His main thing really blocking him is his drug use. It's not beyond him to get up, to be energetic, because I've seen the difference. If he could just get a grip on that, I honestly believe that everything that's out here waiting for him will come full force, if he'd just stay clean consistently because I've seen the three months clean when he was forced what he could do.

"The first time I went to Florida with him he said, I don't care what state you go in, and I didn't know his [addiction] was that bad then, that an addict knows where to go. He said, the first time I came to Florida we went down this street right there… and I've never forgot this… and whenever I go someplace with him, I'm much more guarded. I don't let him get out of my vision because you taught me that lesson you said to me.

"Like he said it started innocently. It was with Earth, Wind and Fire. He had to do it for them to perform and that's how he got started. He said, 'First I would tell them no, but you know, they was getting high, had the stuff on the table.' He said, 'I was doing pure cocaine. It took me a while, but once I got started...'

"You know, I'm not big on bands. And then when there was a chance to get with John, I was like, 'Oh, Lord, are they safe? You know, that's my thing, are they safe?' And then he told me he didn't drink when I met him, and I was happy with that. And I wondered why the band kept wanting him to drink. You mean you're not going to get a drink? The drinks are free tonight.

"I hate to say it but I'd much rather see him drink. If he'd drink, I'd be okay with it. But he's not a drinker. If we could get him in a controlled setting where he'd be safe, he could go far.

"I know it's that horn; he loves that horn. Take that saxophone from Maurice, you have no more Maurice. And next in line would be comedy. Be a comedian."

. . .

Author Interjection:

I watched the romance simmer. Every few weeks either Maurice would bus to Kentucky or his fiancée would drive to Cleveland. At the time of the event he was living in an efficiency apartment on Euclid Avenue just east of Cleveland State. We were scheduled to take photographs and I promised I would pick him up.

I went to the apartment building, took the elevator to his floor, and knocked on his door. A few minutes later, only half dressed, he opened the door to his apartment on the wall of which his fiancée had written "I love you, Saxy." (sic) The bed, which dominated the area when you first entered, had what looked like covers rumpled into a bedroll. Then the "lump" shifted and it was obvious that someone was completely buried in the blanket. "I didn't know your fiancée was visiting this weekend," I commented casually.

"She's not," he said. He didn't smile, look embarrassed, or react in any other way. I dropped the subject and pretended to notice nothing further. A few weeks later, after several years of a long distance relationship, the Sax Man was no longer engaged.

It would be easy to say that the Sax Man was no better or worse than any other entertainer who becomes all too friendly with an ever-changing group of available fans. But there is something different about Maurice. He had talked about the Kentucky woman, regularly expressing surprise that they were still together. He was shown how to use the text messaging on his cell phone, then sent her 140 character love notes in such quantity that he used up his monthly minutes two weeks early much like an adolescent. But Maurice never seems to really want to know a woman, to develop the type of relationship that would deepen with time.

Maurice is too randy to be a monk, too dedicated to playing on the streets to commit to a long term relationship, and too interested in performing to invest time and emotions in meaningful intimacy. It is a disconnect that does not force him to be alone but assures he will likely always be a loner.

.

Chapter Twenty-One

Reminiscence and Thoughts on Music as His Son Encountered it

"The first rappers... well, they call it rapping when you're in jail... They say "we sit around and we rap," you know what I mean. But the cats that did the rapping that could really sing, they were in to another thing. I'd say who really started the rapping thing was Louis Jordan ('Take me right back to the track, Jack') that was rappin' But these cats out here.... And making all that money. And you can't hear nothing. You don't know nothing. Now I'm going to tell you a rapper who should be called a rapper is Johnny Cash. He's a rapper that sings country cause he don't sing, he talks. There isn't no voice there. He really talks. He's like a rapper. On top of these other cats calling themselves rappers and making head-over-heels money. It's just hollerin' it's not trying to educate nobody's ears. There's nothing to educate. Just noise."

. . .

I told my wife to hurry up or we'd be late. She said, "Didn't I tell you an hour ago I'd be ready in fifteen minutes?"

. . .

My wife caught me cheating on her, but I told her, "Darling, you only caught me twice." She said, "I caught you a hundred times. I only told you about it twice."

. . .

Playing in Asia:

The overseas things was beautiful. They totally accepted us there. I've been to Japan three times. The second time I stayed there nine months. I would have stayed longer but the bass player, Jimmy Garrett, who used to be a bass player with Motown, diabetes got him and we had to come back here and he died in New Jersey. The nine months over there, paid very, very well and the people were fantastic. Everybody over there smokes and nobody's got cancer. That's weird, isn't it? I mean, *everybody* smokes and you don't see no fat folk.

"That one time I had a trip with Jimmy Smith. We had been over to Shanghai just for a minute. You talk about people. Two days over there but I noticed when I got over there, they got people just everywhere. Like Osaka, they got people in Japan, but Shanghai got so many people and you never see a pregnant woman. You never see nobody pregnant. France is good. France is beautiful. This last time we went to Lucerne.

240

There they've got four different languages there— Italian and German, and English... Then we went to Bordeaux where they make all the cognac. Cognac factories. We went through all the castles. The people were beautiful. They accept you like everything's cool. No color.

"People were just like Norway, Sweden, Denmark. The people are nice. I don't know if they just treat musicians good or not but they sure did treat us nice in those places.

"I didn't run into too much trouble in my era."

Chapter Twenty-Two

Street Corner Competition —
The Saxophone Territorial
Imperative

A generation later, when the music world was the Sax Man's era, his father settling into a regular gig at Fat Fish Blue, Maurice, Jr. was the only Cleveland musician with year around dedication to the streets. If someone brought him a paying gig in an area club, he was delighted to accept and do his best. But when he finished his sets, he would hurry out the door to play for audiences leaving shows, fans leaving sporting events, and gamblers trying their luck at the downtown Horseshoe Casino. Reedus was not trying to break into any one aspect of the city's music world. He just wanted to play his sax for the world at large, and the streets provided him with both a stage and an ever changing audience.

Had there been only one saxophone player during this time there might not have been tension within the Reedus family. But

Maurice needed to be a soloist and Kelvin needed to learn techniques his relative had already mastered. That was why Kelvin tried, at first, to play on street corners where he might be able to ask his cousin questions. As Kelvin explained:

"I used to play down here in front of the Huntington Bank. I've still got the pictures from the last guy who took 'em. It was some years back. One year we had a seventy degree day in the winter. I was out there in a short sleeve shirt. I think I was playing Eleanor Rigby." And he [reporter/photographer] wrote a little picture article on me, just a shot saying it's so warm that I'm dressed in a short sleeve shirt. Then I get up the next day and Maurice beat me down.

"I said, man, why you going to come down and invade my spot. As good as you play you can play anywhere. I'm just struggling, and the reason I turned you on to all this is because you said you was going to teach me some things. You ain't took no time out with me yet, and still to this day he ain't took no time out to show me nothing. So I just kept going down the road by myself, studyin', playin', trial and error. Fortunately the music theory that I had accumulated while I was in jail that carried me."

Kelvin added, "That's where I'm at now. Music... All I really want to do is just go as far as I can with this music, and I'm regretting now all the time I lost when I was in the joint. I could have been way down the line had I not had those run-ins with the guards. I was just as determined then, especially because I had all the time. That's why I've got the trumpet now cause it's just something I'm determined to finish up cause I had gotten started. I ain't doing too bad on it. I can play all my Mary Had A Little Lambs, Hot Cross Buns, and that there. But I just can't wait until I can come public from it. But that don't take away my affinity for the saxophone."

His affinity and his efforts lasted literally until the day he died.

Chapter Twenty-Three

The Eccentric Becomes a Star

March 14, 2003:

The Odeon in the Flats. Performing was Dredg [sic], the band appearing as part of their El Cielo album tour. Attending, among others, was Cinematographer John Pope.

Pope was one of many visitors to Cleveland events who had heard The Sax Man playing on the street. The sounds had passed over him as another part of city life. That night, though, John was putting the familiar into a new context. "What turned me on about Maurice was the sound of the sax in the city. It was the sound of the sax on the city walls.

"I always associated Cleveland in my mind with a cold place. I don't know what it was. I always think of it in the winter time for whatever reason. It's a very monochromatic city. It doesn't feel like it had much life or color to it.

"I originally was a musician. That's my background. That's where I came from. I'm always paying attention to music. I came up singing. I used to be in a band *Narcissus*. We recorded five albums. We actually had a record deal and all that jazz. We toured, the advanced warp tour. We started in '98 and were together for just about five years. This was way before I ever imagined I'd be a film maker. I always imagined I'd be a physician. I sang in the band, but I'm also a drummer as well. I also play a little bit of piano.

"I remember hearing Maurice quite a few times almost subconsciously. My ex-wife would go up to see shows at Playhouse Square and I vaguely remember him there. And certain times I was in Cleveland for random things I was doing there. Or, I'm trying to remember if we ever played... "We used to play the Flats a lot. The old Peabody's. He might have been around when we played shows at the newer Peabody's.

"What happened the night at Dredg, me and my buddy went up to see the show. They got about three-quarters of the way through their set and all of a sudden they bring this tall black guy up on stage. I distinctly remember his dreadlocks and his lankiness. He was dressed sharp.

"He didn't look like... it's funny because this has been a common theme even to this day throughout the documentary... I remember him dressed nice and not looking like a street musician. He actually looked like a performer.

"And they played the intro, which I already was familiar with when they first started letting their guitars ring. The song is called "Woe Is Me" and that is also off El Cielo. And on the album they actually have a saxophone intro. There's no particular line or chord progression. Really it's just a saxophone that's fluttering and making certain little sounds, and then the song starts. That's the way the album version is, and what they did with this, they actually had Maurice just freestyle something.

"They hooked him up, he played with some sort of delay pedal, and it was awesome. It was just such an incredible improvisational intro. I can't remember if Maurice played throughout the entire song. It was just an intro but it was an extended version, and it was just the performance that stuck with me.

"My gosh, it was so cool! Not only was it that, but it was Dredg bringing him up to actually do some improvisational work, which obviously I respected the band for doing that. What they did was said, 'We'd like to introduce you to our friend, Maurice. We found him on the street and wanted to bring him up on stage for you guys.' They specifically said that.

"Dredg is kind of an out of the box kind of band."

Pope explained that in previous encounters he had become tired of hearing the same songs played over and over again. It would be a familiar complaint by those attending one or another sporting event in the downtown area. Outside the theaters at Playhouse Square Maurice would add songs from whatever show was being performed. He also would take requests, and though he responded similarly at the sporting events, many of those attending the latter had enjoyed from one to several beers. The Playhouse Square was a more reserved crowd, or at least they tended to arrive completely sober. But always Maurice responded to whatever his audience wanted and that frequently meant repetition that convinced some regular sports fans that Maurice was limited in his skills.

John Pope, far more conscious of The Sax Man's potential following the Dredg concert, called himself "disenchanted" with Maurice for doing whatever songs people would reward with tips. The cinematographer seemed to feel there was a selling out, a determination to make money rather than working to expand his repertoire and further hone his skills. "For whatever reason, I think maybe when I first saw Maurice, when I first heard him, I think I was attracted to the spirit of what he was doing and what he still does that comes out from time to time, and the way he was able to get up with that band. It was like there's that piece...

"I'll put it this way, it's actually pretty crazy how this is all coming around to me right now. I was having a discussion over the past couple of days about these guys who go out and do extreme sports. There was a documentary that we were discussing called "The Art Of Flight" and basically a lot of these guys who go out and do it, they are okay with what they're doing and the extremities of it. They're okay with knowing they could die that day doing what they love. It's just in them to do it. There is no question. It's just in them and they're okay with that. They've made peace with that, and they make peace with that all the time.

"With Maurice, I think that it is just in him to do what he's doing. He has made peace. He doesn't know any different."

"It's so much deeper than a routine, in my opinion. I guess what I'm referring to is the artistry of being a musician, of being that kind of musician, it may take different shapes and it may fall into different ruts, but at the core of it, he wouldn't be doing anything else. That's just him. "Back in 2003 when I saw him, other than age, I look back at it now and it's the same. There's something there that really sparked my interest. It was an appreciation, I think, for what he does. I'm no one special. I think a lot of people feel the same way that I

248

do. But as a musician, just seeing the way he interacted with. It was a special moment. One of my favorite bands interacting with this free spirit... It just got me going and it stuck with me subconsciously.

"That night he got off the stage after the song. It's like he just came and went. The crowd loved it and he had to return to the streets."

"Now I saw him from time to time. There was another moment when I got a cell phone number. It was 2008 was my next interaction because I was just finishing up school. I went to school for audio composition and ended up switching at the last minute because I discovered film making. And about that time I was just getting started.

"I think I saw him after a Keane concert. Keane was like a pop/rock piano trio. I want to say they played some rib burn off thing. It was in the summer.

"I saw Maurice and I said, "I'd like to come up and shoot some video of you sometime. I don't know what to do with it, but it would be really cool to just shoot you playing your sax."

"He got all excited. He mentioned one of the reporters for Channel 5 and said, 'He got an Emmy for doing a spot on me. News Channel 5. Yeah, yeah you do a piece on me.'

"He gave me his cell phone number and I put it in my cell phone. And I remember thinking 'this is awesome!' Maurice Reedus... Maurice Reedus, Jr.

"Anyways, Joe [Siebert] and I had been working together at Stone Kap [Productions].

"I was working some job with Joe when we were working at Stone Kap together. I remember being like, 'Hey, man, I met this guy up in Cleveland.'

"Whatever reason I keep coming back to him in my mind. There's something special. There's something special about him. I just want to follow it. I just want to explore it a little bit further even if we just do a short documentary like a couple of minutes just shooting this guy. Just me and you. I'll shoot it. You direct it. Maybe Derek (the other camera operator) why don't we go do something?"

The "something" became a trade-off. The company for which the young men worked was one that produced commercials, short documentary type stories, and related industrial products. They also took on personal projects on their own time, and it was in this category that they saw Maurice.

Joe's heart was in a short, seven minute documentary called *The Real Bold Badmen* about two cowboys from Canton, Ohio, who used to make westerns. That documentary was a short, and John thought the same type of production would work well with Maurice. He was the only one who saw the possibilities that day but he did gain Siebert's cooperation to serve as writer/director on what would become *The Sax Man* project.

Pope later commented, "If someone had said, 'Why?' I would just have to say that that was just what was inside my gut. I was led to go talk to the guy. There was a voice inside. That sounds crazy. People say that's creepy or weird.

"There was some kind of enigma there.

"I worked on a short stint of a documentary that was done on [singer] Marilyn Manson. It was for AMC [American Movie Channel] it was for like Rockumentaries or whatever.

"I actually met Hugh Warner, his father, and we did an interview with him, a cousin, a couple people from the area. But I talked with the producer after the shoot and she was telling me that they had already done the interview with Manson and she's like, what a crazy, weird guy. I mean, granted, a lot of the drugs—I guess he's a pretty huge coke addict—probably God knows what else, I mean a lot of those big musicians are...

"And the thing was, you talk about these people, how eccentric they are. Maurice... He's just one of them who never made it to the big time, but he's still like that eccentric... He's like that guy you'd talk about like, Man, that Maurice, he's a cool dude but he's weird. He's very strange.

"I think he made it to the big time. I think he passed through the big time and really has no concept of that.

"He has no concept of the space and time. He's just doing his thing... I don't know. It's wild."

. . .

But Wait a Minute...

For more than three years I spent time walking the streets with the Sax Man. I photographed him playing on Public Square and Playhouse Square, outside one or another sporting event, outside one or another concert venue, performing on East 4th Street as it transitioned to a food and entertainment draw for people living far beyond the city. I was introduced to police officers who knew his name but had never talked with him. I was introduced to comedy headliners at clubs in the Flats and on East 4th Street who also knew his name, though they, too, had never talked with him. I heard developers and politicians warmly greet the Sax Man, though they did so in passing, never lingering more than a minute. And I met the women who loved him but with whom he had never truly shared his feelings, his hopes and his dreams. I talked with people I noticed watching the Sax Man's performances, especially on Public Square where, in nice weather, he "owned" the lunch hour, well- dressed Clevelanders choosing to ignore the area restaurants in favor of carry-out they could eat on benches while they listened to Reedus.

Then there were the coffee shop managers who made certain Maurice had a sandwich for his efforts. And there were the Playhouse Square Red Coats, the ushers who observed all that took place between curbside drop-offs and getting straggling audience members to their seats. Finally there were the loyal fans, an eclectic group of the disabled, the unemployed, the downtown residents, and the shoppers playing hooky from a slow day in their business offices. Most stood to watch. A few brought folding seats on which to rest for so long as he was playing. And one woman used a digital camera as she shared her extensive knowledge of music and musicians she had seen in traditional concerts. Some called him "Sax Man." Some called him "Maurice." Nobody seemed to have ever had a personal conversation with him in the past, and they certainly did not during the time I was observing what was taking place.

Then there were the people who could only be called fans such as two women who walked to wherever Maurice was playing, setting up a stool for one of the women to use while the other took a digital camera and photographed the Sax Man. She was also a serious music fan who could discuss the work of a number of performers she had seen though usually in concert, not on the street.

Just out of ear shot it seemed as though everyone was willing to express an opinion about Maurice, including myself when I first met him, but no one had really talked with him. Interviews done by one or another television station, either on the street or in the studio, were innocuous—how long have you played on the streets? You're out there every day? You're a Cleveland icon, aren't you? Would you play something for us on the way out to our commercial break?

No one had taken him to a coffee shop or restaurant to learn what his life had been like growing up, the type of friends he had, how he became involved with music, his family's activities (Among other professions within the Reedus family there is a school principal, a professional football player, a New York media personality, and of course his father, a Grammy winning musician.). Maurice was either the black sheep or the star, depending upon how the listener might value his eccentricities, yet no one talked with him.

Maurice loved the media appearances. He loved the feeling of being special, of everyone knowing his name, of being told by strangers that they had seen him on television, heard him on the radio, or found his picture in either the *Cleveland Plain Dealer* or the *Akron Beacon Journal*. He was thrilled when a mural of Playhouse Square was painted between the entrance level and the lower food court level of the Halle Building. Looking closely at the mural as you ride the escalator there is a very obvious, albeit impressionistic, image of the Sax Man playing his horn.

There was more. I went into music stores with Maurice, then returned on my own to talk with the owners who also had never really spoken to Maurice though they knew how and where he performed. I witnessed the Sax Man at his low points musically when he had to make emergency repairs on his sax by using heavy duty rubber bands. I witnessed him without a desperately needed reed when he entered a music store, then discovered he no longer needed a reed when he was back outside.

Part of Maurice seemed brilliant, determined, and taking delight in bringing pleasure to strangers. Part of Maurice had what one fellow musician who had known him for decades called "sticky fingers." There seemed to be an odd morality to the Sax Man's actions. Those times I learned he had been stealing, the objects could be justified as being critical for his work. After all, the thinking might have gone, how could he pay for reeds even if they only cost 50 cents or a dollar each if he didn't have a reed with which to play so he could earn the money to legitimately go into the store and buy the necessity.

Sometimes Maurice explained his plight to the dealer, and a few would "eat" the cost or find a way for him to work off what he owed for the needed items. Other times they would work a discount others did not receive as a way of helping. And a few just noted that he never kept his word about paying for the item when he made money again.

The Sax Man always seemed to have a sense of personal entitlement to whatever he needed, yet he was both without arrogance and without a sensitivity to the feelings of others. It was as though he considered his music a selfless gift that others would recognize, then reciprocate by allowing whatever he needed so he could keep strolling the streets, keep filling the night air with the sounds of his saxophone.

The other negative that marked his activities was the occasional use of one or another stimulants to push himself to perform when his body was exhausted. Certainly there were occasions when I watched him go from exhausted but determined to a brilliant performance I would have thought he was too wasted from lack of sleep to handle.

Even as I began writing and rewriting this book, the delays it caused certainly frustrating for the publisher, I realized that the Sax Man had become like a Ken Doll manufactured by the Mattel Toy Company. Just as Ken comes fully clothed in a box with see-through lid indicating what type of play he is ready for and cluing in the buyer as to what additional clothes he will need, so The Sax Man comes with different suits, different berets, but one consistent saxophone case. He will always play the saxophone (Though Congas can be arranged—$1,000 and up a set). He'll always dress as though he's about to go on stage and wants to show his audience the professional side of him. And he'll always be Barbie's favorite, though The Sax Man presumably arrives anatomically correct, something that cannot be said for Ken.

It is easy to joke about Maurice. He is a loner, living and working in isolation but fantasizing that being daily in the midst of thousands of Clevelanders wherever he plays is the same as actually having an interpersonal relationship with them.

The Sax Man is also as insensitive in his personal relationships as he is sensitive to his fans on the street (when he stops long enough to really see them, hear them, and respond to them). He finds the love of a woman on a regular basis, sex with a woman a little more frequently, and seems surprised when either the woman he loves leaves him or he drifts apart from her. He considers himself a hard man to live with, then admits that womanizing is the primary cause of those he loves walking away from him (or getting fed up and telling him to get lost.).

Still, in many ways everything keeps coming back to The Sax Man as a Ken Doll.

Those who were aware that his choices have not always been the best express frustration and/or anger when he is banned from a store or faces a minor shoplifting misdemeanor charge. At the same time, they recognize his is not so much a life adrift but a life with but one primary focus—playing his saxophone for all who will listen. He is insensitive to the rules, lifestyles, and values of others, not in an arrogant way but not seeing them as a part of his world.

The documentary that was being shot through 2013 brought much of this into sharp focus, though ironically the documentary crew missed the real Maurice. They created what amounted to a staged life, projecting their values and beliefs onto the Sax Man (the Ken Doll, again). He had had two high points in his career. The first was the Kool Jazz Festival, though that was so many years earlier it could not be of great importance to the film. There was little, if any, affordable film stock of the event. Instead, the high point was the night the Cleveland House of Blues had an opening ceremony (ironically the same time as the Christmas tree lighting ceremony on Public Square when Santa made his first Cleveland appearance of the season.), Both Maurice, Jr. and Senior were on stage along with Dan Ackroyd, the actor who was in a number of films including *The Blues Brothers*, having ridden to the event on a motorcycle in the midst of a contingent of Hell's Angels.

It was a dramatic night, an exciting night, and if a period of time can be considered eccentric, it was as eccentric a time as the Sax Man's lifestyle. Equally important, he was so thrilled with the honor and the experience shared with so many other regional and national greats that he frequently wore the back stage pass he had received even when months had passed.

The film crew for the documentary considered that event a dramatic high point of the Sax Man story. They saw a man who played for the opening and then, for the next several years, had only played outside. He had never again been on their stage. That was why they decided to stage a reunion concert with Maurice and many of the top musicians with whom he had played when younger. It was a dramatic story arc. It would make an exciting finish. It would bring tears to the eyes of the viewer. And it was wrong. That might work for the Ken Doll. It was not the story of the Sax Man.

Chapter Twenty-Four

But What about Tomorrow?

As 2013 progressed and news of the Sax Man documentary spread, reaction seemed to be mixed. One music store owner was outraged by the publicity. He felt that there were young musicians with far greater talent and ability who would have loved to play on the streets of the city but avoided doing so because of Maurice.

The reasoning was never all that clear. Did they feel they could not compete with the high standards set by the Sax Man? Did they feel that there were few places to perform and competition by even one musician would make their ability to earn money near impossible? Or did they feel that Maurice was such a limited professional that if he represented what Clevelanders wanted to hear on the streets, they would go where *real* music was appreciated?

What Maurice's detractors seldom discussed was how the

reaction to the Sax Man's work actually made earning money on the streets easier for everyone. Most Clevelanders either enjoyed hearing him play or ignored him. However, among the "haters" were a couple of police officers who tended to hassle Reedus when they were directing the crowds outside the Indians' games and he was on East 9th, playing as people passed on their way into the stadium. He was arrested more than once and was ticketed twice in 2013 for not having a peddler's license and not having a vendor's license. What the officers either did not know or did not care was that neither license was needed. Maurice and any other busker who was playing music and accepting tips but not panhandling, not demanding money, not creating a physical danger to passers-by where he was standing was within his legal rights.

It was difficult for Maurice to know where to go to complain about his treatment. He had no idea if the charges were valid under the law, though he assumed they weren't. And to be truthful, the sense of entitlement he seemed to carry meant that he would have argued with his treatment even if he was wrong and knew it.

At the same time, honesty compels the reminder that Maurice has never been an altruistic angel beatifically embracing the people of the city. He can be hot headed (though never physically violent) when experiencing sugar highs and lows from a diet that seems to consider cookies one of the major food groups. He can be belligerent to authority (though never his public) when exhaustion and a need for income leads him to buy an illicit stimulant to get through the next few hours. And he has been banned from more than one store because of his "sticky fingers."

Cleveland is a town as famed for the number of county lead-

259

ers, employees and business people who have gone to jail for bribery—both giving and receiving—as it is for its world class medical centers, arts organizations, museums, and symphony. Maurice's troubles with retailers and the law usually have involved amounts not as great as a dinner once cadged by a county commissioner. It is easy to ignore the petty when there are federal prisons that could easily have their own former Clevelander booster clubs.

The problems Maurice was having were topics of bemusement for the documentary crew. They were putting together a reunion concert bringing Sly, Slick & Wicked to the House of Blues for a reunion concert with Maurice and several top professionals with whom Maurice had played over the years. At first the producer wondered if they would have to somehow "paper the house," bringing in an audience who, if truth be told, would watch anything for a free ticket. They were also concerned about publicity—would he show up for early morning news shows? Would he attend all rehearsals? And when he lost his apartment, would he be able to find a place to live?

Maurice, for his part, seemed to be rebelling against everyone who he rightfully felt had been using him. He needed a place to live but lacked the money required to rent an apartment. He had no savings and could not pay both a month in advance as a deposit, the usual requirement. He had become eligible for low income housing through Cleveland Metropolitan Housing Authority (CMHA) but though that was immediately affordable, nothing was available in the near downtown area where he needed to live for his work.

Perhaps there would be some form of assistance available to him. Perhaps if he went to one or another agency an arrangement could be made. But Maurice told no one of his dire circumstances. His mother had made very clear before her death that he was not to go to his sisters who apparently would have helped him. She wanted him only going to her, a demand he respected, neither expecting her to die.

The only answer seemed to be to take a room in one of the inexpensive hotels serving the Cleveland State University campus. The management gave him a special low rate and a room that had a small stove and refrigerator. Even with that, he found himself owing more money per week than he had ever earned on the streets. And because he told no one why he was there, the production company personnel assumed his new-found fame had gone to his head. He had plenty of money. He wanted for nothing. Asking them for help was a way of whining and they didn't want to hear him whine. They did give him $500 at some time in the summer, bought him an occasional meal when they were stopping to eat, and contributed towards one day's rent on occasion. But there was no steady payment for his time, a fact that made him feel the documentary was a waste of time, the fame seemingly hollow.

Maurice never thought about why no one came forward with cash for him. Most of the people he knew could not afford to help him, were just getting by themselves. Others, perhaps including the production personnel who had raised at least an estimated $250,000 specifically to tell his story, saw no reason to help what at least one decided was a drug addled former professional musician whose body would probably be found in a gutter one day. "You can't give Maurice a bunch of money," I was told. "He'll just waste it on drugs or something." It was a justification based on nothing. Oddly, it was Maurice's late mother, or at least some of his mother's words, that changed his life at that moment. Scared, often hungry, most of his possessions taken and destroyed by his former landlord who evicted him without following legal procedures and going through the courts, the Sax Man realized he could no longer act the cute little boy who could wheedle Mommy into being the seemingly unlimited "Bank of Mom." He was on his own. He had reached the age of 60. He had spent four decades developing whatever skills he had. He was a man who had to take responsibility for his life in a manner that had never happened before.

Maurice, tired, stressed, went on the streets with his saxophone. He mentally plotted the layout of the downtown area, planning where to play. Were Broadway shows in town? That meant playing on Playhouse Square in the hour before the curtain rose for each show taking place that day, then returning for another half hour or so when the show was over and the audience was coming out to the streets.

Was it a nice day with office workers taking advantage to go to lunch at various fast food restaurants and moderately priced coffee shops? That meant Public Square was his concert hall or, on truly warm days when people liked to eat outside, he might try East Ninth Street between Superior and St. Clair.

Was there a sporting event? Basketball was just starting, but football meant that many of the fans were drunk by the time they reached the stadium entrance and their generosity seemed unlimited. The same was true when they exited, tipping well because the team had won and tipping well following a loss because they seemed to want to make at least one person happy after the game.

Then there was the Horseshoe Casino, the excitement of gambling in a space at once beautiful, exciting, and without windows or clocks. 24 hours a day passers-by on the outside might tip the Sax Man for luck, tip the Sax Man to brag about how well they had done, tip the Sax Man because it was their last few dollars and they seemed to figure, what the hell... It was better to tip the guy making music who was giving them more pleasure than the last few throws of the dice or pulls on the slot machines.

Little by little Maurice was earning the money to pay for his room. He might be a few hours late or have the cash a few hours early. What mattered was his mother who he was convinced was looking down on him from Heaven, guiding his actions. When he worked the way he knew he had to in order to succeed, everything seemed to go his way. He was approved for the apartment and could be told a move-in date at any time. He was eating, and though that often meant junk food such as package cookies, it sometimes meant a friend dropping by and leaving him a Subway sandwich. In desperation, Maurice "The Sax Man" Reedus was gaining self-respect.

. . .

For the documentary crew the reunion concert they arranged to put on in the Cleveland House of Blues was the highpoint of their show. Maurice had played in House of Blues when it opened and he stood with his father, actor Dan Ackroyd, and numerous other greats while 800 people cheered. Then, in the months and years that followed, he had played only on the outside, an itinerant musician and not a star. Having a reunion c o n c e r t with him dominating the show would be the story arc—no riffs, no flourishes, just beginning to end with the Sax Man.

The concert may have seemed the Coda of a musician's life, what the Italians call the tail, they were wrong. Much of the evening was tense despite a paying audience that filled the venue and was a surprise as to the types of people who attended.

First, the audience skewed older—perhaps in their forties or fifties on up into their seventies. Second, they were mostly white, another surprise. And third, they knew the songs, from *Surely*, the first hit by Sly, Slick & Wicked, to what, when many in the crowd would have been teenagers, to what in the 1950s and early 1960s would have been branded as "race music."

[For those unfamiliar with the type of music once dismissed as "race music," this was never in any way similar to the type of urban rap songs filled with anger, violence, and foul language. These were songs about chaste love between teenagers whose parents often did not understand them or the depth of their feelings about the boy/girl in their life. Comedian, author, composer, and late night variety show host captured this world—both white and black—with his satirical lyric: "Once we were young and foolish. Now we're 13 and in love." The songs could only be described as sweet, gentle, and perhaps achingly naïve—more "bubble gum pop" than ghetto hard.]

The production crew thought Maurice wanted to be famous, and the publicity certainly skewed in that direction. They thought he longed for the time when he was a star, his music, blended with the rest of the band, delighted audiences that often numbered in the hundreds, as in the Cleveland House of Blues, or in the thousands, as was the case with the various summer jazz festivals. They fantasized that he had reached stardom of sorts when he played for the opening of the Cleveland club and returned to stardom with the show both featuring and honoring his work.

. . .

Mayor Jackson Proclaims July 18th "The Sax Man" Day in City of Cleveland—Street Musician to be Recognized at House of Blues Concert

Cleveland, Ohio—July 15, 2013—Cleveland Mayor Frank G. Jackson has issued an official proclamation that will make Thursday July 18th "The Sax Man" day in the city of Cleveland. In the Mayor's proclamation, Maurice Reedus Jr., better known to Clevelanders as "The Sax Man," is recognized as an "iconic street saxophone player who has long been a symbol of positivity in the city."

The proclamation will be presented to Reedus on stage at the House of Blues this Thursday, July 18th. Reedus will be performing an once-in-a-lifetime reunion concert with his old Motown band—Sly, Slick, & Wicked.

"This proclamation is a blessing and a true honor," said Reedus. "I love Cleveland and can't wait for the people to see my show with Sly, Slick, & Wicked. It's been almost 40 years since we've played together and no one in Cleveland has ever seen me play like I'm going to play this Thursday night!"

The concert will be filmed as the final scene of "The Sax Man," a

265

feature length documentary about Reedus' life being produced by local filmmakers. People from across northeast Ohio are invited to come out to the show for their opportunity to be in the film and show their support on "The Sax Man" day in Cleveland. Mayor Jackson also used the proclamation to encourage the citizens of Cleveland to "join him in recognizing The Sax Man's contributions to the culture of Cleveland, and thanking him.

. . .

I looked at what was taking place and realized that the audience was dominated by men and women who had likely been forbidden to listen to WABQ and WJMO, the only Cleveland stations giving them regular air play, when they were entering their teen years. Certainly the music would not have been played at their school dances (Yes, the musicians had played for such gatherings, but they were black, the schools they attended were predominantly black, and white kids were too rare at such events to account for the audience's ability to sing every song performed. It was a little like looking at a gathering of old former revolutionaries singing the words to songs few realized they had learned.).

The musicians were brilliant, Maurice showing his skills with the Congos along with two other former Courageous Young Men. I finally understood that the Congos were very much the Sax Man's first instrument and one he had truly mastered beyond any possible criticism.

The music, the applause, the excitement certainly matched the thinking about the end of the film when it was edited and narration added where necessary. There was also intense tension, the musicians feeling that some of the production staff did not respect them, did not give them credit for what, in some cases, was a half century of performing. At one point when John Wilson was being arrogantly lectured about proper music, timing, editing, and other factors, he quietly explained that he had scored a half dozen full length, major motion pictures in his career and was continuing to do so. This was the lecturer's first since graduating from school.

There were also moments during the show when a crane brought into the club space was either not being handled carefully or was deliberately swung towards Wilson. He had to quickly move out of the way to avoid being seriously hurt. He was convinced the action was deliberate on the part of the operator. What was equally likely was that the operator of the $10,000 piece of equipment either did not have the time to practice or did not take the time to practice. Either way, tension was high among those involved with coordinating and filming the production.

There is no question that Maurice was thrilled with what was taking place. But while the documentary makers and others saw the moment as the high point of the Sax Man's life, and they were probably right from their perspective, Maurice quietly uttered words few, if any of the others present, heard him speak. He looked at what was taking place. He listened to the talk of an after party. He accepted hugs and handshakes from performers he hadn't seen for decades until they were reunited during rehearsals. Then, before he returned to his hotel room and a television set for company, he was heard quietly saying, "But what about tomorrow?"

Chapter Twenty-Five

A Room of One's Own

I never learned the financial arrangements for Maurice's participation in the documentary about his life and work. He and others had the impression that the documentary crew, which had raised backing of almost $250,000 by the night of the show with his former band, was providing him with next to nothing. There was a $500 payment several weeks before the House of Blues Sly, Slick & Wicked show, and there were nights when one of the principals or crew paid his rent for a night. But he was both the least compensated and the only person who was fighting to stay in even a small apartment.

By the night of the show, many people were impressed that Maurice was living in a university area hotel in a room that had a small oven and refrigerator meant for use in both extended stay, inexpensive hotel rooms and efficiency apartments. The cost was $60 a night, $420 a week, an outrageous sum for a man with no savings and no predictable source of income.

Some of the members of the production company were

shocked. Did the Sax Man not have more sense and better judgment? Why not take all that money and rent a real apartment? Why does he say he needs anything? And the unkindest comment: "You can't give Maurice money because he'll just waste it."

The truth was harsher and, as with the fact of his dyslexia, something he wanted to keep hidden, an embarrassment and a circumstance that brought him great sadness. Maurice had been evicted from the efficiency apartment in which he had been living because he could not keep up with the rent. He might earn enough in any given couple of weeks to be able to meet his obligation, but he could not set aside funds from a good night to cover a bad one. Everything was fine over time, but the sporadic nature of his earnings made the cost of an efficiency beyond his means at any given time. It was either a hotel or a shelter, and the shelter was likely to be more dangerous than the apartment where the landlord not only evicted him (illegally it appears because proper filing and notice had not been made) but trashed his possessions.

And his mother in heaven:

Maurice was suddenly faced with the loss of most of what he valued. Some possessions, such as a photo I took of father and son playing in Fat Fish Blue, can be printed from the negatives and enjoyed for years to come. Others, such as a picture of his mother he began carrying with his sax whenever he played, are probably also held by family members who can get new prints made. But little things to others, such as a Spiderman doll, may not be available despite its personal importance [Cleveland has become a growing motion picture production region and the casting directors know that if they want a roaming busker on the streets of Cleveland/New York/Gotham or any other fictional urban setting, Maurice always meets their needs. He may not be seen. He may not be filmed except in the midst of a crowd whose presence overshadows him. But if a sax is heard, Maurice is blowing. The doll in question was one of his souvenirs from his time on the city/set].

For many weeks, Maurice had been seeking to rent an apartment operated by Cuyahoga Metropolitan Housing Authority, the agency handling low rent housing. Once Maurice was on the list, his goal was to get an apartment in the near downtown or downtown area. Then, when his circumstances elevated him to a next available apartment status, he was given a list of buildings in the area where he wanted to live and told to check them out. And among the vacancies was the Ernest Bohn Apartments just off Euclid Avenue and a five minute stroll to Playhouse Square's theater district. The rent would be roughly half of what he was trying to pay at the hotel, and instead of owing by the day, the rent would be monthly, a sum he not only could afford but one that would assure he would no longer have to choose between eating and having a decent place in which to live.

Almost as important, Maurice had to work harder than he had ever worked before. Some of the people who knew Maurice were outraged that he was living in a hotel. They had no idea that he usually started each morning with no food and no cash with which to buy any.

For years Maurice had relied on his mother to keep him off the streets when he didn't work as hard as he needed to in his chosen career, or when he wasted his money on non-necessities. He had ignored her advice, sometimes respecting it and other times just not listening. After all, he was almost 60 years old, too old to be treated like a little boy. Yet he still relied on her to hold an unusually large sum of money usually earned when playing before a football game where a jovial, heavily liquored-up crowd kept dropping $5 and $10 bills into his case, or before a sold-out show by a Broadway touring company. His actions seemed responsible and his mother duly praised him, but both knew that much of it would be spent on cigarettes and package goods—cookies and the like—that had long ago rotted his teeth.

Suddenly everything changed. His mother had long ago insisted that he not approach his siblings for help in getting by. She made clear that any help he received should come from her, though whether that was to keep her son from becoming a burden to the rest of the family or to assure he would remain beholden to her was not known. She also seemed to be the type of person who would seemingly live "forever," certainly outliving Maurice, Jr. yet she died. There was no emotional preparation, probably no thought that his life could radically change.

Maurice, Sr. was also dead, of course, but their relationship had never been about survival. There was intense grief over his loss, a man who had long been an idol, a role model, a personal hero and inspiration. But the older Reedus left recordings behind, music that his son set about mastering. Knowing he was on his own when he walked into the hotel, and though they were kind enough to his plight to reduce the rate they normally charged their guests, he still needed more money than he had ever earned from the streets of Cleveland.

The answer was to follow what he perceived as his mother's teachings from when she was alive and her guidance from Heaven now that she was no longer alive. He walked the streets in a pattern that assured encountering the greatest number of people who might appreciate his efforts. He went to East 4th Street with its combination of restaurants, a comedy club, and other attractions all topped by one and two bedroom apartments. He went to the entrance to the Horseshoe Casino, playing for the winners, the losers, and the newly arriving hopefuls. He went to Playhouse Square before and after show times, and he went to Public Square to catch people at lunch and others going home from work. He went to the Flats and he went to the cluster of bars and restaurants on West 6th and West 9th Streets. He walked. He played. He stopped. He played. And if he rested, it might only be for a couple of hours at a time. He also avoided looking to buy the type of stimulant that had turned Gladys Trice away from a music career.

And Maurice paid for his hotel room. Maurice bought food, though friends, proud of what he was doing, would sometimes drop by with a Subway sandwich or other carryout item.

But he paid for his room, a fact that shocked even his family. The daily obligation required him to work the streets for hours, something he had never done with such tenacity before. He performed with the intensity of the most serious of buskers and the public favorably responded. He was like a high wire circus performer, the safety net that had been his mother was no longer in position to catch him. Maurice's less than desirable circumstances could still be viewed as a triumph, and the combination of the honors he had recently received with the knowledge that he was acting more maturely than perhaps at any other time in his life changed the Sax Man. Not long after the House of Blues show Maurice was asked to perform two numbers at the first annual R&B Hall of Fame Inductions, a night when John Wilson was one of the first of the honorees.

I expected nothing special when the awards program began. Various groups performed. The inductees were shown along

272

with a short video covering their careers and contributions to R&B music. This was interrupted by a number of young and older performers including Maurice.

Suddenly the sound of a saxophone could be heard as Maurice "Sax Man" Reedus strolled out from stage left. He was quiet, casual, moving among other performers, gently moving his horn from side to side like a lasso encircling both the notes and the listeners, gradually bringing them together until they blended as one and the auditorium was filled with the Sax Man's music. Then, as he came to center stage, he explained that his father's favorite song had been *Route 66*, one I had heard the older Reedus perform at Fat Fish Blue.

Maurice held his horn and began singing about getting his kicks on Route 66. His voice was mellow, smooth, showing no hint of damage from the endless smoking of cigarettes. It was a sound and a style that would have delighted a cabaret audience and totally unexpected from the Sax Man. And when he was finished, he continued his stroll off stage.

"Your theatricality was brilliant," I told Maurice the next day. "From the moment you started your stroll onto the stage, you owned that audience. It was the most exciting work I've ever seen."

"I just tried to remember what my father would have done and then I did the same."

"No, that's not true," I told him. "I've seen your father perform several times and this is nothing like his work. This was uniquely you and it was fabulous. You were brilliant."

The Sax Man knew I was serious, knew I believed what I was telling him. He turned his head away, said nothing, and I watched a tear slowly form at the corner of his eye.

Chapter Twenty-Six

The Finale is the New Beginning

I stopped by the hotel when Maurice learned he would soon have full approval for an apartment in one of the Cuyahoga Metropolitan Housing (CMHA) apartments where his monthly rent, adjusted for his assured income, meant that he would be paying less than the cost of the hotel per day. He was tired, tearful, and joyous, convinced that his late mother hadn't left him in death but was guiding him from Heaven. He talked about how he was finally doing all the things his mother had tried to teach him over the years, and the result was the greatest success he had experienced on the streets of the city. Each day that he paid his rent seemed like another triumph; one in which his mother had her hand. In his mother's death he had found the greatest closeness.

And that's when the real end of the Sax Man's story became evident. This was not a traditional life's song with an exciting overture and tragic Coda as his critics believed and his friends feared. This was the beginning of a second chance, one riff blending with another, an old song becoming new.

The joy came because the Sax Man knew he had finally earned a home, a place to rest, a base from which to walk the streets of the city serenading the rich, the poor, the young and the old, a permanent address from which to get hired by bands doing short term tours of clubs throughout the region and throughout the country. The hopes and dreams of a 19 year old kid who surprised even himself by earning his chops at the top of the profession were again to be fulfilled, this time by a man four decades older and most likely for the rest of his life.

· · ·

Cue the Announcer:

Ladies and gentlemen, the musician who plays before an estimated *five-million* office workers, sports fans, and theater enthusiasts every year, a former star at the Kansas City Royals stadium where his horn blasted through the air at the 1975 Kool Jazz Festival, a back-up musician for the internationally known Sly, Slick & Wicked, has now committed to the streets of the city of Cleveland, Ohio, for what will be a lifetime contract.

Maurice Reedus, Jr., a flawed genius whose entire life has been lived in on-key and off-key riffs and flourishes, is setting down roots. The city that has kicked him, cursed him, feted and embraced him yet always remained his most faithful lover now welcomes him home for the rest of his life.

www.ingramcontent.com/pod-product-compliance
Lightning Source LLC
Chambersburg PA
CBHW022003090426
42741CB00007B/874